The Malaysian Albatross
A Collection of Literary Essays
on the May 13 Incident

The Malaysian Albatross

*A Collection of Literary Essays
on the May 13 Incident*

SIM Wai Chew & TEE Kim Tong, *editors*

國立中山大學人文研究中心
Center for the Humanites, NSYSU

離散／現代性研究室
Diaspora | *Modernity*

The Malaysian Albatross:
A Collection of Literary Essays on the May 13 Incident
Edited by Sim Wai Chew & Tee Kim Tong

ISBN: 978-626-95583-4-6

First Published October 2023 by
Diaspora/Modernity Cultural Research Unit
Center for the Humanities, NSYSU
National Sun Yat-sen University, No. 70, Lianhai Road
Gushan District, Koahsiung City 804
TAIWAN

Diaspora/Modernity Cultural Research Unit
Center for the Humanities, NSYSU
Essays by the authors

Printed and Bound in Taiwan by
Sin Wang Pai Co. Ltd
1Fl., no. 163, Andong Street
Sanmin District, Koahsiung City 807
TAIWAN
886-7-311250

For those who still believe in
Malaysian Malaysia

INTRODUCTION
May 13 and Its Post-memories

SIM Wai Chew

"Everything in Malaysia is champor-champor […]"

——Shirley Geok-lin Lim, *Joss and Gold* (2001)

OVER half a century has passed since the watershed events of May 13, 1969—the series of politically spurred racial riots that left hundreds dead in Malaysia's capital, Kuala Lumpur, forced the resignation of its then prime minister Tunku Abdul Rahman, and instigated a two-year lapse in parliamentary rule. Its effects continue to ramify in the socio-politico arena. The ushering in, in the name of national security, of a rash of policies that effectively institutionalized a reified ethnie-based order. Mahathir Mohamad's 1991 invocation of "Bangsa Malaysia" ("Malaysian nation/race") as a counterweight to the social exclusion partly normalized by that institutionalization. The entrenchment of a complacent, self-serving elite and the rise of the "Bersih" or "Clean" movement questioning egregious abuses of power. These and other developments it may be argued are directly or indirectly the consequences of the fractiousness unleashed on that fateful day.

Not surprisingly perhaps, the fiftieth anniversary of the event in 2019 prompted calls for a public re-assessment and review. The activist and educator Kua Kia Soong, for instance, called for the establishment of a commission to examine disputed aspects of the riots, not least the official death count of 196 which he contended was grossly understated.[1] In order to get a clear picture of what transpired, public institutions such as hospitals, the army, the police and the Special Branch should be made to declassify their files, Kua argued. Only then would a modicum of "reparation" be made to families of the victims; and only then would Malaysia get to "exorcise" its many May 13 revenants.

Unlike the, so to speak, buried records mentioned above, delineations of May 13 in Malaysia's cultural archive subsist obviously in the public realm but are not particularly well understood or appreciated. As a representational trope, it is an elephant in the room: unmissable certainly, but also unaddressed or discussed. The essays gathered in the present volume attempt to make up for this shortfall. Collecting in revised form English-language papers delivered at a May 2019 bilingual conference held at the National Sun Yat-sen University in Kaohsiung, Taiwan, the volume raises some overdue questions about the impact of May 13 on Malaysia's arts and letters. Similar questions are posed by its companion volume which gathers together Chinese-language essays presented at the conference. In combination, the two collections ask and proffer answers to the following. How do writers limn and understand the event and its aftermaths? If May 13 highlights the dangers of ascriptive cleavages, can its aesthetic delineation help to foster cohesive diversity? Are there generational differences in the understanding or interpretation of the event? Do writers of different ethnic background approach the issue differently?

As the conference was the only academic event held anywhere in the world to commemorate the fiftieth anniversary of May 13— a small coterie of the Malaysian intelligentsia diaspora in Taiwan having kept alive the enquiry—these two volumes constitute the only standalone work offering critical deliberation on how the event

---

1   Kua Kia Soong, "Time to Declassify the Secrets of May 13," *Free Malaysia Today*, 12 May 2019 (freemalaysiatoday.com/category/opinion/2019/05/12/time-to-declassify-the-secrets-of-may-13/).

operates as post-memory in Malaysia's national imaginary. As such, they augment in a timely and judicious manner its postcolonial cum pluri-cultural formation. Nevertheless, the lack of sustained work in the area means it can only initiate a conversation or dialogue. What the editors hope is that, with the publication of the collection, their conversation about May 13 will be joined by other scholars interested in the topic, that through both consensus and dissensus an improved understanding of its implications and significance will be achieved, and, most importantly, that the deliberations conducted therein will facilitate intergroup accommodation.

In the first essay below, Shirley Geok-lin Lim, lamenting the rupture of "national communal relations" represented by May 13, devotes considerable space to delineating the hybrid Sino-Malay ("Peranakan") lifeways which she counts as her inheritance and birthright. For her, the tragedy of May 13 amounts to the aborted development of peranakan culture as indexed by folk songs and children's verse cherished not just in Malaysia but also Singapore and Indonesia. Because that identity was "complexly combinational"— making room for Malay, localized forms of English as well as other tongues—it operated as a template for multicultural development and contained in nuce the promise of Malaysia. For the more au fait reader, this feeling of missed opportunity is perhaps itself complexly combined with knowledge of Lim's own May 13-initiated diaporan journey and her subsequent evolution as a notable voice in Asian-American letters, a development that gives, as it were, an external "wing" to Malaysian literature. Despite the nostalgic hue of a piece that is part wounded testimony and part critical reflection, however, Lim is hopeful about the new autochthonous forms of pluralism that have arisen in recent years in Malaysia. If earlier forms of pluralism lacked "postcolonial self-reflexivity" and thence suffered from Eurocentrism, the hope is that the new "recombinant" forms will avoid those pitfalls.

In the second essay, Malachi Edwin Vethamani examines a slew of English-language works that touch on May 13 including Lim's own *Joss and Gold*, Lloyd Fernando's *Green is the Colour*,

Preeta Samarasan's *Evening is the Whole Day*, and Hanna Alkaf's *The Weight of Our Sky*. Apart from novels, Vethamani also discusses plays by Lee Joo For and Jit Murad, poems by Ee Tiang Hong, Ghulam Sarwar Yousuf, and Bernice Chauly, and short stories by Karim Raslan and Paul Ganaselvam. Identifying the affects limned by these works—affects that range from dark humour and remorse to lament, fellow-feeling, perplexity, and fear—he observes that while some "unscrupulous" politicians reference May 13 to garner ethno-popular support, "Malaysian writers" tend to display "caution and sensitivity" when addressing the topic; they do so not because of extant censorship laws but because they are effectively charting "a way forward" for the nation, a way that "heal[s]" the wounds caused by the event.

Following on from the focus on Malaysian Literature in English (MLE), the next two essays by Florence Kuek and Sim Wai Chew use the methods of comparative literature to probe the issue at hand. Kuek surveys thirty-two works published between 1969 and 2019 written originally in English, Chinese, and Malay, all of which touch on May 13 in one form or another. She argues that works produced by ethnic-Malay background writers are "prescriptive" in nature, displaying ethico-pedagogical commitment to causes such as "national unity" and "racial harmony" or conviviality. Ethnic-Chinese writers in contrast tend to be "descriptive": their works elucidate negative valence emotions such as "grief" and "agony" and also evince a "post-traumatic" fixation on events intensely cathected as "post-memory." To flesh out her claims, Kuek discusses in greater detail a novel (*Interlok*) and a short story ("Melissa") written by national laureate Abdullah Hussain. She also discusses works by Ding Yun and Looi Yook Tho (Lu Yu Tao), as well as the young adult novel written by Alkaf mentioned above. In the case of *Interlok*, Kuek observes that while it doesn't directly employ the May 13 topoi, it does engage "honest[ly]" with the historical provenance of intergroup hostility in the country, namely the "divide and rule" policies initiated by Britain, Malaysia's erstwhile colonial ruler.

Sim on his part examines recent MLE and MLC (Malaysian Literature in Chinese) works with an eye on the critical-theoretical exigency bequeathed by May 13. Given the hypostatization of ethnic-being, it would seem that critics have to find forms of collective life that can ameliorate social fractiousness. In the context of eco-crisis, Sim argues that conservation and-or place-sensitive epistemologies elaborated in works by K.S. Maniam, Chuah Guat Eng, Li Zishu, and Hai Fan aids that larger effort. To designate the issue at stake, Sim offers the term polyculturalism, which he takes from Vijay Prashad. Unlike multiculturalism, which stresses separate spheres of living, polyculturalism spotlights overlapping interests, projects, and concerns. Under its imprimatur, Sim proposes a return to the cultural archive to uncover modes of relationality needed for a politics and aesthetics of collectivity.

Finally, it bears repeating that the dialogue furthered by this volume will hopefully foster the growth of pluralism and cohesive diversity in Malaysia. If the historically-sedimented, everyday reality of the formation is that, as the epigraph above puts it, everything is "champor-champor" (jumbled up and impure because of the mix of cultures), then it behooves all denizens to recognize their essential imbrication in a community of fate. Apprehended in this manner, one might argue, the only practicable response is a fusion of horizons that seeks to overcome tension and discord.

The Breaking of a Dream
May 13th, Malaysia

Shirley Geok-lin LIM

I was twenty-four years old on May 13th 1969, when racial riots broke out in Selangor, chiefly in the Malaysian capital city, Kuala Lumpur, and its suburbs. Although *Wikipedia* terms the violence "Sino-Malay sectarian," every historical source notes that most of the massacred and injured were Malaysian Chinese.[1] I was then living in such a suburb, near the University of Malaya campus, and a postgraduate student working on a Master's degree in the Department of English, in the only university then in Malaysia.

---

1   See "13 May Incident" in *Wikipedia*. Kua Kia Soong presents an empirically drawn history in his book, *May 13: Declassified Documents on the Malaysian Riots of 1969* (Kuala Lumpur: Suaram Komunikasi, 2007). While Kua's publication of just then declassified British and other foreign records of the May 13th events has been criticized by some as partial, it is the only extant historical recounting of the violence, as Malaysian records have never been shared and are said to have been destroyed. See also Baradan Kuppusamy (2007): Dr. Kua "blamed then-deputy prime minister Abdul Razak and others for engineering the May 13 violence and subsequent coup which brought down Malaysia's old order. 'The riot was just a backdrop to seize power,' he said. [...] [D]ispatches, between the [British] mission in Kuala Lumpur and London [...] showed that [...] the all-Malay army units stood by and let the mayhem happen. [...] One British Foreign Office document dated May 15, 1969, succinctly concludes that the riots were organised to 'formalise Malay dominance, sideline the Chinese and shelve the Tunku's government.'"

Prior to May 13th 1969, Malaysia had been newly pieced together as a political state, composed of the Federation of Malaysia that had achieved independence in 1957, united with North Borneo, Sarawak and Singapore. However, the perceived threat of voting outcomes in upcoming elections, that Singapore's majority ethnic Chinese urban dwellers would undermine Malay numerical superiority particularly marked in the rural hinterland, lead to fears of Chinese ascendency and resulted in Singapore being unceremoniously kicked out of Malaysia in 1965. The ejection of Singapore from Malaysia post-dated the establishment of the University of Malaya in Kuala Lumpur in 1962, when a tolerant multi-cultural and multilingual educational policy governed. These historical contexts alone may explain why I, like so many of my friends, thought everyone in our elite university were Anglophiles. With no postcolonial self-reflexivity, English teaching assistants taught tutorials on British poetry, from Shakespeare's "My mistress' eyes are nothing like the sun" to William Butler Yeats' "Easter 1914." The twelve years after Merdeka appears now like an interregnum in a Twilight Zone, we young colonized English-language-loving zombies sucking the blood still from a separated fantastical dead motherland called England.

My poem "Monsoon History," composed sometime in the 1970s while I was negotiating a *fugit tempus* diaspora in the United States of America, figures a child raptly reading Lord Alfred Tennyson's poems. This British colonial education shaped for me an imaginary that is both a specific historical moment in my Malaysian sensibility and simultaneously an alienation from that particular geospatial locale. Because "Monsoon History" was taught over many years as part of the Malaysian Fifth Form English Literature curriculum, it has been interpreted as iconic of my growth as a Malaysian Anglophone poet. My present poetics, however, perhaps would have owed as much to *Peranakan* [native-born] verse had May 13th 1969 never happened. It was never "Tweedle Dum and Tweedle Dee" that amused this *anak* [child] in my mother's house, for my *Emak* [mother] recited no Mother Goose verse, no "Pat-a-cake, pat-a-cake, baker's man," no "Mary, Mary, quite contrary" to her children. In fact,

Emak's English was quite weak. Unlike my *Hokkien*-speaking father who had studied in British-run schools till he was seventeen and who enjoyed reading English-language newspapers and magazines like *Time* and *National Geographic*, *Emak*, who had stopped schooling at twelve, hardly read, and instead loved a good gossip and laugh, both shared in Malay, her mother tongue.[2]

Some anthropologists speculate that *Nyonyas*, Malay-speaking *Peranakans*, are descendants of the Batak tribal women who married the *Singkeh* immigrants from Fujian. *Batak* women undertook the ancestral worship rituals their foreign husbands demanded. Not Muslims, rather like the Hindu Balinese, they ate pork. Skilled in the fiery curries and *lemak* coconut dishes based on the freshest of local herbaceous ingredients, costumed in elaborately filigreed figure-hugging *kebaya* sarongs handed down by their foremothers, their descendants devolved to Chineseness without losing their original indigenous language and socio-cultural practices. These social acts included, on auspicious occasions, chewing *sirih*—a quid concocted of betel leaves, areca nut, lime, gambier and cloves— and strict observations of female modesty, coupled with a dominant matriarchal family structure. In my mother's household, till I was eight, I was raised a *Peranakan* female. When my mother gave up her children, she was admitting the failure of her interracial marriage, between a patriarchal Chinese and a *Peranakan* matriarch, a family unit weakened, then wrecked by material desires and economic booms and busts coming out of subordination to colonial forces apprehended only as a distant West.[3]

Like my parents' marriage, my childhood oral poems, in contrast to those I read in books imported from Britain, were a mix of English and Malay with some *Hokkien*, this linguistic mix being in actuality our home language. Our mother tongue was not bilingual; rather, it

---

2   *Hokkien* is an oral dialect of Chinese that has shared roots with the dialect from Fujian that has many similarities with Taiwanese Chinese.

3   I have written at much greater length of my fraught childhood and my parents' marital troubles in my 1995 memoir, *Among the White Moon Faces: An Asian-American Memoir of Homelands.*

may in hindsight be taken as fully a Manglish orality. Here is a poem we chanted-sang in the same way that British children might have chanted-sang "Mary had a little lamb."

> Sitting under the *pokok kelapa* (coconut tree)
> I will sing for you.
> Oh Mina, kiss me *lah*,
> Don't *tutop pintu*. (close the door)
> Your face is like a *pinyapu*, (broom)
> Your curly hair is full of *kutu*. (lice)
> Oh Mina, my own, own sweetheart,
> I love you, *selalu, sanghat*. (always, very much)

Occasionally, we sang folk songs that were completely in Malay, as with "*Chan Mali Chan*":

> *Di mana dia anak kambing saya?*
> *Anak kambing saya yang makan daun talas.*
> *Di mana dia buah hati saya?*
> *Buah hati saya bagai telur dikupas.*
> *Chan mali chan, chan mali chan*
> *Chan mali chan, ketipung paying.*
>
> *Di mana dia, anak kambing saya?*
> *Anak kambing saya main di tepi sawah.*
> *Di mana dia, cinta hati saya?*
> *Cinta hati saya yang pakai baju merah.*
>
> *Chan mali chan, chan mali chan*
> *Chan mali chan, ketipung payong.**

> *Where is he, my little goat?
> My little goat is eating taro leaves.
> Where is he, my loved one?
> My loved one is like a shelled egg.

Where is he, my little goat?
My little goat is playing by the paddy fields.
Where is he, my loved one?
My loved one who is wearing red.

Where is your little goat, sir?
Sir, your goat is on top of the bridge.
Which one of those is your favourite flower, sir?
It is the Tanjong flower at the end of the branch.

If you want to know where my goat is,
It is in my room.
If you want to know which is my umbrella,
It is the tiniest one.
Where is your goat, sir?
Your goat that has yellow fur.
Which one is your loved one, sir?
My loved one is the one who's in white and yellow.

When I heard this folk melody played over the Air Asia plane
on my flight from Kuala Lumpur to Penang in November 2018, a
rush of homesickness stunned me like a wave knocking me off my
feet that I had not expected rushing from a horizon I had forgotten to
check for safety. Today, in the 21st century, Air Asia publicity office
has shrewdly played on Malaysians' identity sentiments that are
Malay-lingual-rooted, easily roused, easy on the ear, and communal
in the extreme, shared by almost every Malaysian national flying on
Air Asia, whatever his or her ethnicity.

Some other song lyrics, claimed also by Indonesia and
Singapore, are "*Burong Kaka Tua*" [Old Tutok Bird] and "*Rasa
Sayang Hey!*" The last in my childhood memory serves as a kind
of anthem for my mother's people, harmonizing on "the taste" or
feeling of love:

Rasa sayang, hey! Rasa sayang sayang hey,

Hey lihat nona jauh, rasa sayang sayang hey.
Rasa sayang, hey! Rasa sayang sayang hey,
Hey lihat nona jauh, rasa sayang sayang hey.
Buah cempedak di luar pagar,
Ambil galah tolong jolokkan,
Saya budak baru belajar,
Kalau salah tolong tunjukkan.*

*I feel love, hey! I feel love, love, hey,
Hey, when I look at that girl, I feel love, love, hey.
I feel love, hey! I feel love, love, hey,
Hey, when I look at that girl, I feel love, love, hey.
The jackfruit is outside the fence,
Please take a stick and poke it down,
I'm just a new guy trying to learn,
So if I'm wrong then please show me the way.

Despite the gendered lyrics, this folk song was sung lustily by both boys and girls, men and women, absent the melancholic, sexual yearning, romantic address to a loved one that dominated Western Tin Pan Alley records that played on our radios, as in "Red Sails in the Sunset" or Nat King Cole's "The Falling Leaves." In my Malacca childhood, *"Rasa Sayang Hey!"* was an unself-conscious campfire song for Boy Scouts and for multiple-generation church picnics.

Like the insertion of different DNA segments to form new recombinant chromosomes, *Peranakan* language plays, as seen in these examples, arguably modeled a multicultural nation-identity evolution not drawn from a single-race-origin but complexly combinational. The May 13th 1969 racial violence, arson, and killings of hundreds or even thousands of innocent citizens, leading to the yet-to-be repaired rupture of national communal relations, achieved a traumatic wounding of a generation of unique Malaysians who learned and sang Malay and English language songs with equal fervor and *sang-froid*. May 13th marked the extreme shift from probable recombinant nation-evolution, as instantiated in these linguistic examples, to reified, or even apartheid, raced identities. After May 13th, after the blunt imposition of Bahasa Melayu as the national language and the marginalization of the then medium of instruction, English, as well as of Tamil, Chinese, and other ethnic languages, to sectional, that is, subordinate status, the kind of playful orality that characterized *Peranakan* speech became politically fraught.

Stigmatized as bazaar Malay or pidgin English, serving neither as a marker of Chinese ethnicity or of educated professionals working in Bahasa or English-language offices, the fusing of Malay and English registers termed Manglish is sometimes viewed as parallel to Singlish which many Singaporeans delight in claiming as a major feature of their national identity. However, Singapore and Malaysian Englishes are distinctively differentiated, the way that non-identical twins possess differentiated features. Singlish, albeit with some official resistance, is now widely accepted as the home language of Singaporeans, the comfort tongue of the nation. However, in Manglish's recombinant DNA, Bahasa is the foundational corpus; in Singlish, it is arguably *Hokkien*. Also, despite what has been noted about features shared between Manglish and Singlish, Manglish does not possess the socio-cultural, even state-recognized, legitimacy of a home-language that Singlish enjoys.

Beginning with my generation, the split between Malay and English language writing in Malaysia is overt, evident, chronic, and seems no longer redeemable. Muhammad Haji Salleh, despite his 1970's outspoken and celebrated rejection of English language writing to commit to what he argued was an authentic national Malay language literature, now quibbles and obviates between composing in Malay but also almost simultaneously translating into English. He explains his present shifting positionality in his 2000 essay "Rowing Down Two Rivers,"[4] in which he juggles seemingly incommensurate

---

4   Muhammad Haji Salleh, *Rowing Down Two Rivers* (Bangi: Penerbit Universiti Kebangsaan Malaysia); also in "Decolonizing: A Personal Journey," he argues that writing only in English is a "sin" (2000a: 60). He continues to equate Malaysian national identity with the Malay language. As critics have noted, "Muhammad is a strong advocate of this policy of nation formation, in which all the Malaysian

goals, between Malay prideful ascendency and individual authorial ambition for a global readership, abjectly accessible only through the once-abused "bastard" English language.[5] Today, Chinese-language Malaysian writing is read only by Chinese-educated Malaysians, and its translation whether into Malay or English appears incapable of crossing over to other Malaysian language communities.

A social analyst might study the historical and current tensions and debates in Malaysian literary production as on-going symptoms of a post-traumatic-stress-disorder on the body of the nation. Before May 13th, communal relations and political discourse assumed a merit-based, non-raced ethos; after May 13th (and the passing of the New Economic Plan—NEP—, emphatic sedition laws and new Constitutional amendments), non-merit, race-based-hierarchical, Malay-supremacist social and governmental structures were enforced as the new normal. This new normal, in place for half a century, is all a couple of generations of Malaysians have experienced, but PTSD symptoms have recurred through these years after the race riots and massacres, to remind many Malaysians that there once was a different national identity-ideal that the new normal denies.

races are expected to embrace and rally around the Malay language": "I gave up the colonial language to write in the national language. For the time being I would like to see writers contribute their talents to a literature in this [Malay] language [...]. That will solve the problem. Writers should have a sense of roots, national identity and pride in their language" (Mohammad A. Quayum, 2006). In the 2019 interview, he repeats: "Malaysian literature, by definition, would be the literature written in the national language. It is a literature in progress, now being written by not only the majority Malays but also by the Chinese, Indians, Kadazandusuns, Ibans, Bidayuhs, Bajaus and the Aslan (first) peoples. We have many interesting works from East Malaysia, with unique cultural backgrounds and use of language. This is a richness that is also being discovered. Together, all these writings will be the Malaysian literature" (Nursafiri Ahmad Safian & Mohammad A. Quayum 127).

5 I have critiqued M.H. Salleh's "ambivalence," shuttling between an overt insistence on the evils of a multilingual literature (which he argues subverts "Malaysian" national identity)—grounded on his unswerving equation of "Malaysian" literature as ONLY literature written in Malay—, and his rationale that translating his poems into English and writing his critical essays in English in no way contradicts his position that English is a colonial and thus "bastard" language. See my "English in Malaysia: Identity and the Market Place" in *Asiatic* (Lim, 2015); and also his recent interview with Nursafira Ahmad Safin and Mohammad A. Quayum in *Asiatic* (2019), which repeats these contradictions.

PTSD is widely diagnosed as "an anxiety disorder that some people get after seeing or living through a dangerous event. When in danger, it's natural to feel afraid. This fear triggers many split-second changes in the body to prepare to defend against the danger or to avoid it" ("Posttraumatic stress disorder"). May 13th 1969 initiated a mass exodus of Malaysian citizens to Singapore and territories more distant. Currently, there is some public discussion on the relation between the unrecorded loss of lives on May 13th and the on-going loss of many more thousands of citizens since May 13th 1969, under the euphemism of "brain drain." Lim Teck Ghee asked, "Was May 69 the watershed or is it simply one of several past tipping points [...] ?", and answered "[T]he roots go back to not only 1969 but also to the change in educational policy in 1970 requiring students sitting for the MCE to pass Bahasa Malaysia or they would not be able to get entry into local universities. The period after this educational policy change saw the out-migration of non-Malays and their children pursuing their studies abroad begin in earnest." In short, he notes the almost covert perception that Malay supremacy evidenced in "institutional racial and religious discrimination and individualised experiences as push factors for those who have left the country or are seeking to leave" (Lim Teck Ghee, 2019).

Whatever the reasons, records coincide to support that with each fresh flashback rousing anxiety and fear, a fresh flood of Malaysians exit the body politic, either physically in a global diaspora or psychically, withdrawing from political and civic engagement to supposedly safer narrow communal concerns. That is, many Malaysians exhibit avoidance symptoms, "staying away from events that are reminders of the experience," hence the continued historical erasure of that date and its aftermath, with no annual notice of the event, the perpetrators, victims, memorials or site markers of physical violence and damage, no estimates of fiscal costs to national wealth, losses to individuals, families and businesses, no Commission established to arrive at answers to any of these issues. If one were to raise May 13th to even intimate friends, the first reaction often is to deny its significance to contemporary Malaysian society;

that is, Malaysians express emotional numbness in response to this historical event, another symptom of PTSD.

As to how different ethnic communities feel about the trauma, because there is no public sharing, one cannot conclude if any Malaysian may have felt strong guilt or depression after May 13th. But fears this trauma may recur are ever-present in the sedition laws and the absence of social discourse on the event. The nation has moved on, one may infer, except that erasure and silence that rule any May 13th discussions are symptoms not of recovery and healing as of repression and denial. In the place of memory and healing, the nation is continuously displaying hyper-arousal symptoms of PTSD. Public discourse, whether political or academic, has been clearly tense or "on edge" whenever race and its unspoken companion, violence, are referenced.

Re-experiencing symptoms of the May 13th trauma, I argue, include flashbacks. Medically, flashbacks occur when the trauma is "relived over and over and includes physical symptoms such as elevated heart rate and perspiration." In similar manner, whenever threats are raised by some ethnic groups of race violence in the event of unacceptable actions by other groups, the May 13th trauma is relived even without recourse to overt references to the historical event. See, for example, the recent incident reported at the *South China Morning Post* of 20th March 2019, of a "Malay power" neo-Nazi band festival that was cancelled in Malaysia's Ipoh city. The article notes that many of the Malay heavy metal bands preach a "'Malay power' movement, that Malaysia should be an exclusively Malay nation, immigration should end and non-Malays should be expelled" (Wright, 2019). The photograph of a crowd at a Boot Ax performance shows young Malay men in Western tees doing the Nazi salute. These Malay power bands have names such as Xenophobia, Spiderwar and Total Distrust, English words that denote explicitly extreme Malay supremacist positions. The article quotes an interview with the pop culture website *Vice*, in which Slay, a band member of Boot Ax, explained the Malay power movement as "concerned about keeping a pure Malay community all over the Malay Archipelago."

"Malaysia is home to people from China, India, and foreign immigrants from Bangladesh, Africa, Sri Lanka, Nepal, and Burma [Myanmar]," Slay told *Vice*. "The government can't control the entry of immigrants, and we get so many of them." Valorizing Nazi ideology, Slay adds, "The lesson that we can learn from Nazism is that we can take extreme racist action if the position of the Malays is affected by these factors." These Malay supremacy groups of educated youths openly articulate anti-immigrant sentiments, collapsing anti-Malaysian-Chinese and other ethnic-Malaysian-citizens communities under this umbrella immigrant rubric, to threaten violence and even killings (as suggested in the naming of the band's spokesman, Slay). Any anti-Malay statement would rightfully result in immediate arrest of the speaker under the strict sedition laws, yet these Malay Power bands have free access to multimedia platforms and have not been arrested for inciting racial hostility.

The appeal of Nazi idealogy to these Malay Power bands may be explained by the analysis of the motive for the recent massacre of over 50 Muslim immigrants in Christchurch, New Zealand, on March 15th, 2019, by an Australian right-wing white supremacist. As Slay notes, the sentiments of members of his band, Boot Ax, are similar to "blue-eyed" Nazis a century ago. Pete W. Singer observes, "Another tactic they [white nationalists and Islamic terrorists] use is offering a sense of fellowship. It's a strange but very real combination of finding a community and finally feeling understood and appreciated, but they're finding it through the expression of hate" (Campbell, 2019).[6]

The public response to flashbacks raised by covert allusions to the May 13th trauma is fear, resulting in "re-experiencing symptoms" that "may cause problems in a person's everyday routine." Malaysian citizens are easily startled and made anxious by any news related to race tensions and conflicts; at the same time, Malaysians in advantaged race positions are prone to "angry outbursts" if they believe the lessons learned through this historical trauma are being

---

6   See Charlie Campbell's extended essay in *Time*, on a white supremacist's massacre of Muslims in Christchurch (2019).

forgotten. That is, even as the May 13th massacres cannot be openly accessed or studied, it must also never be forgotten. Repression is an on-going effort at memory control, both for ensuring civic peace by surface forgetting and oppressing likely oppositional elements by hyper-arousal of covert or barely disguised anger and fears. According to medical observations, "hyper-arousal symptoms are usually constant, instead of being triggered by things that remind one of the traumatic event. They can make the person feel continually stressed and angry." The overwhelmed Malaysians turn to modifying their behavior, to subdued quiescence, changing the subject, even to thoughts of leaving the country or sending their loved ones away, a form of self-destruction of Malaysian identity.

PTSD symptoms displayed in the national body can occur in weird moments of flashbacks, hyper-vigilance, and on-going wounding. Malaysian society appears "normal," but what now is considered normal is what has been normalized. The Constitution, post-May 13th, has normalized—that is, legitimated—a half century of ethnic or race preference, officially tagged as "Bumiputraism" and often boasted of as Malay supremacy, aka, *Melaya Ketuanan*. According to *Wikipedia*: "*Ketuanan Melayu* (Jawi script: كتوانن ملايو; literally "Malay dominance") is a political concept emphasizing Malay preeminence in present-day Malaysia." Hence, for me, returning "home" usually once a year has been increasingly challenging, for I see what Malaysian citizens have become inured to. To be "at home" is challenging, for I have to turn a blind eye to race-preferences instated through state apparatuses such as public education and universities, government agencies, banks, religious sites and buildings and governments-linked corporations, even so-called private entrepreneurial enterprises, where administrators, staff, faculty, personnel and students are one race majority over-represented. One must squint to not see the on-going depredations on civil service and socio-economic equality brought on by the processes of NEP in the aftermath of May 13th.

But while these explicit repercussions are seldom critiqued and despite on-going episodes of racial hostility, under the scabs may be discerned some healing. This healing remains discreet, an open secret not to be addressed else it invites violence to maintain fear and enforce humiliating displays of submission. Take, for example, the figure of Malaysia's foremost elder literary figure, a poet who began publishing in the 1950s, who has written plays, reviews and essays, and whose many books, all written in English, include his translations of Classical Chinese poetry and rich allusions to Western classical literature like *Antigone* and canonical British poets such as T.S. Eliot. Wong Phui Nam's reputation is established as a major author in Malaysia and with Singapore poets, and critical chapters on his works proliferate.[7] Yet critics do not address the aporia in his texts, that Wong converted to Islam decades ago in marrying a Malay woman, and this long happy marriage has produced Muslim children who are taken as fully Bumiputra. Neil Khor in his 2008 article, "Malacca's Straits Chinese Anglophone Poets and Their Experience of Malaysian Nationalism," makes the case for Wong's liminality as neither a Chinese nor an at-home Malaysian, but Khor's brief biographical note on Wong's marriage to a Malay serves no analytical factor in his psychological reading of Wong's poems (Khor, 2008). Wong's poems and essays, after all, make no reference to this autobiographical matter. Wong's texts do not inscribe or even covertly suggest Chinese-Malay tensions, themes that the seven-generation Malacca *Peranakan Baba* poet, Ee Tiang Hong, directly foregrounds in his pre- and post-May 13th poetry.[8] Is Wong's erasure of autobiographical Chinese-Malay intimate relations a deliberate masking of what is too sensitive for his words to approach? Or does what Wong avoids in his writing represent a void, a "lack" in which

---

7   Wong Phui Nam's six publications, all in English, span over 40 years and include *Anike* (2006), *An Acre of Day's Glass: Collected Poems* (2006), *Against the Wilderness* (2000), *Ways of Exile* (1993), *Remembering Grandma and Other Poems* (1989) and *How the Hills are Distant* (1968).

8   As I noted in 2015 *Asiatic*, of Ee Tiang Hong's oeuvre, "despite his immigration to Perth, Australia, in 1972, [Ee] remains a noted diasporic Malaysian poet, perhaps because he continued writing out of his quarrels with Malaysian identity politics even in his later books, which includes *I of the Many Faces* (1960), *Myths for a Wilderness* (1976), *Tranquerah* (1986) and *Nearing a Horizon* (1986)."

such tensions and contradictions—e.g. his limning a nostalgia for Chinese-language Tang lyrical sentiments while in the position of a Muslim paterfamilias in a wholly Bumiputra family—are "disappeared," rendered mute and invisible because so restrictively contained? And should we take Wong's figure as the foremost living Chinese Malaysian Anglophone poet as an instance of racial passing (passing as Malaysian Chinese or not passing as Bumiputra?) or of racial healing that is not yet ready to be acknowledged?

I give you a second more personal instance. On September 23rd, 1996, I was invited to give a lecture, "Writing a Malaysian/American Memoir," at the International Islamic University in Petaling Jaya by the Head of the English Department, a white American woman who had converted to Islam when she married a Malay poet, who had published an article on my memoir, *Among the White Moon Faces*, and who was teaching the memoir to her undergraduate classes. A question and answer session followed my talk. As is customary in Malaysian universities, only faculty asked the questions. One was raised by a middle-aged man sitting toward the front of the long seminar table while the students were ranked in rows toward the back of the room. I repeat his words almost verbatim: "Lady Professor," he began, "I am from Syria. I have just come to this country and I don't know much about Malaysia, but this is what I see. The Chinese here are very money-minded." He continued in this vein, his words seeming to invite my response to his anti-Chinese statements. I was so taken aback that I did not observe how the other teachers responded to his racist stereotyping. Making an effort to be polite, I thanked him for his question and added, "But your comment is an insult to Malays as it assumes that Malays are not money-minded. There are many Malays who are very successful businessmen, who are CEOs of large corporations. Many Malays wish to succeed in making money; they work very hard to compete and many are doing very well and have become rich. You seem to say they have failed in business because only the Chinese are money-minded." He was silent after my rejoinder, and the faculty moved on to other issues. At the end of the Q&A, a line formed chiefly of students to have me autograph their memoir copies. As I signed and chatted with each, several of them whispered, "My mother/grandmother is Chinese." They did not elaborate what such information suggests of their identities or of their unspoken response to the anti-Chinese stereotype the Syrian professor had confidently thrown out. However, I understood their communication of shared Chinese descent as a silent rebuttal to the Syrian's racism that no faculty beside myself had openly resisted that morning.

It may be argued that a very different narrative may be told of Malaysia, that fifty years of peace, of no repetition of the killings, arson and violence after the May 13th trauma, are themselves proof of healing; that the prosperity that has lifted the boats of every ethnic community (albeit unequally) in this half century is evidence of the success of NEP policies; that democratic ideals of free speech, equality and meritocratic justice are culturally specific Western concepts not suited to particular non-Western societies. Quiesence and prosperity may thus be taken as national goals that unite Malaysian citizens; and thus, the open corruption that ruled in the decades of Najib's Barisan government which threatened Malaysian properity and which disturbed the quiesence of submission to Barisan politicians finally brought Najib and his cronies down.

The stunning victory of the opposition party, Pakatan Harapan, on May 10th 2018, however, does not signify a transformation to a different normal, for free speech, equality and meritocraic justice are still absent in the new ruling discourse. After the Christchurch massacre of Muslims, a sweeping generalization about what unifies New Zealanders as citizens is that although "The indigenous Maori people make up more than a sixth of the population, but they are joined by the descendents of British colonialists and more recent arrivals from the South Pacific, Europe, Asia and Africa. The diverse population is united by shared values of affability, self-deprecating humor and sports" (Campbell, 2019). As a visiting diasporic Malaysian, I do not live in the everyday interactions of ordinary Malaysians, whose coexistance appears to be rather like those claimed for New Zealanders: affable, tolerant, and respectful.

Besides, my perspective is skewered by distance of time and space. But the politics of quotas heavily favoring one ethnic community over all the others remain the foundation of post-May 13th Malaysia, and so long as this *Melayu Ketuanan* continues, Malaysia remains to me yet a traumatized nation, split between an overt ruling body part and other parts bound in unspeaking fear.

The multiculuralism that *Peranakan* Malaysians displayed pre-May 13th is lost forever. Instead a Malay-dominant recombinant culturalism dominates in the 21st century Malaysian nation, one not grounded on genetic purity or even on social practices—see, for example, the "Westernization" of Malaysia in the popularity of heavy Metal music, the increasing numbers of women in the professions, the tastes for Western cuisine, the dependence on Western technology and use of social media, etc; even a more relaxed acceptance of the importance of English for instruction, international business, and communication across ethnic groups—but on religious identity as Muslim.

The voluntary intimate sharing from at least five International Islamic University undergraduates that long ago September has remained fresh with me through the years. I wonder where these students are now; what professions they have gone into, and how they negotiate the racism that simmer daily in Malaysian lives. For me, their whispers of inter-ethnic marriages offer a vision of healing under the scab of May 13th ethnic separatism, a generation of offspring with Bumiputra recorded identities yet also of Sino- or Tamil- or Caucasian-descent, a recombinant DNA authentically Malaysian. These children now grown and perhaps with children of their own are 21st century *Peranakans*, possessing both Southeast Asian indigenous AND Sino or Caucasian or Indo descent lines: the way that some of Prime Minister Mohammad Mahathir's forebears had come from South Asia, the way that certain Sultanates have British parentage, the way that Mrs. Wan Azizah Wan Ismail, married to Anwar Ismail, and the current Deputy Prime Minister, "has a *Peranakan* Chinese grandfather," "but was raised Malay Muslim" (according to reports).

Neil Khor's analysis of three Malaysian Anglophone poets, of whom only Wong Phui Nam chose to remain in the country, views Ee Tiang Hong and myself, both Malacca *Peranakans*, as avowing a multiracial Malaysian identity that was aborted after May 13th. It seems to me rather that while it is a political fact that *Peranakans*— native-born Sino-descent citizens—have been refused recognition as Bumipuras, a status offered to Eurasians—mixed-race citizens who trace descent from Portuguese/Dutch/European colonialists—a new "Malaysian" identity has evolved in which Malay now forms the national foundation ethno-identity (unlike *Peranakans* like myself where Sino is the founding ethno identity), together with Indian, Caucasian and Chinese strands in the recombinant DNA of many contemporary and even more future Malaysians.

A survivor of the New Zealand massacre, Ahmed, notes that "More terrifying [than the killings] was the flurry of cheers and gleeful comments online racists attached to the murderous scenes. 'We underestimate the power of hatred,' Ahmed says" (Campbell, 2019). The unarguable lesson taken away from May 13th 1969 is the same lesson Ahmed teaches us after the massacre of his compatriots while they were at prayer in their mosques in Christchurch, that we take away from the massacres of Sri Lankan Christians on Easter Sunday this year, from the massacre of black Americans in their historic Charleston church by a U.S. white nationalist in 2015, from the concentration camps and gas ovens that were set up all over Europe in World War 2, that for good or for ill, we humans must never underestimate the power of hatred.

WORKS CITED

"13 May Incident" (2019). *Wikipedia* (en.wikipedia.org/wiki/13_ May_incident).

Campbell, Charlie (2019) "The New Zealand Attacks Show How White Supremacy Went from a Homegrown Issue to a

Global Threat." *Time*, 21 Mar. (time.com/magazine/south-pacific/5555848).

"Ketuanan Melayu" (2019). *Wikipedia* (en.wikipedia.org/wiki/Ketu anan_ Melayu).

Khor, Neil (2008) "Malacca's Straits Chinese Anglophone Poets and Their Experience of Malaysian Nationalism." *Archipel*, no.76: 127-149.

Kua Kia Soong (2007) *May 13: Declassified Documents on the Malaysian Riots of 1969* (Kuala Lumpur: Suaram Komunikasi).

Kuppusamy, Baradan (2007) "Politicians Linked to Malaysia's May 13th Riots." *South China Morning Post*, 14 May (www.scmp.com/article/592766/politicians-linked-malaysias-may-13-riots).

Lim Teck Ghee (2019) "Brain Drain and the Role of the State." *The Sun Daily*, 5 May (www.thesundaily.my/opinion/brain-drain-and-the-role-of-the-state-KI846963).

Lim, Shirley Geok-lin (1995) *Among the White Moon Faces: An Asian-American Memoir of Homelands* (New York: Feminist Press).

Lim, Shirley Geok-lin (2015) "English in Malaysia: Identity and the Market Place." *Asiatic* 9.3: 1-25.

Mohammad A. Quayum (2006) "On a Journey Homeward: An Interview with Muhammad Haji Salleh." *Postcolonial Text* 2.4 (www.postcolonial.org/index.php/pct/article/view/458/456).

Muhammed Haji Salleh (2000) *Rowing Down Two Rivers* (Bangi: Penerbit Universiti Kebangsaan Malaysia).

Muhammed Haji Salleh (2000a) "Decolonization: A Personal Journey." *Journal of Commonwealth and Postcolonial Studies* 7.2: 51-67.

Nursafiri Ahmad Safian & Mohammad A. Quayum (2019) "Malaysian Literature and Its Future: An Interview with Muhammad Haji Salleh." *Asiatic* 13.1: 119-141.

"Posttraumatic Stress Disorder" (2019). *Wikipedia* (en.wikipedia.org/wiki/ Posttraumatic_stress_disorder).

"Wan Azizah Wan Ismail" (2019). *Wikipedia* (en.wikipedia.org/wiki/ Wan_Azizah_Wan_Ismail).

Wright, Adam (2019) "'Malay Power' Neo-Nazi Band Festival Cancelled in Malaysia's Ipoh City." *South China Morning Post*, 20 Mar. (www.scmp.com/lifestyle/arts-culture/article/3002515/malaysian-neo-nazi-bands-lined-kuala-lumpur-concert-similar).

The Malaysian Albatross of May 13, 1969 Racial Riots

Malachi Edwin VETHAMANI

Introduction

RACIAL riots in Malaysia are an uncommon phenomenon though there is a constant reminder and threat that the 13 May 1969 riots could recur. The 13 May 1969 racial riots remain a deep scar in the nation's psyche even today and the fear of such a re-occurrence continues to loom especially when some unscrupulous Malay politicians remind the nation that such an eventuality is a possibility if the privileged position of Malays is threatened. Yet, Malaysia has prided itself as a model for multi-cultural and multi-racial harmony in its sixty over years of existence as a nation. However, its attempts at forging a Malaysian race of "Bangsa Malaysia" (Mahathir 1992: 1) has not been achieved. In recent post colonial nations, especially in nations with mixed populations like Malaysia, a lot of effort is put into projecting a national culture or a national identity. This attempt to forge various races into a single cultural entity is an impossibility, and it is a misconception that there can be a single national culture. As Ahmad says, any nation comprises cultures not just one culture. He asserts that it is a mistaken notion that "each 'nation' of the 'Third World' has a 'culture' and a 'tradition'" (9).

This paper examines Malaysian writers' creative response in the English language to the 13 May 1969 riots. It presents a brief historical context to the violent event and political response to the event which has resulted in the passing of various policies and laws that has impacted not only on the re-structuring of Malaysian society but also the management of the relationships among the multi-ethnic communities in the country. Andaya and Andaya state that, "Malaysia's post-independence history treats 1969 as a watershed that marks the beginning of a new era in the country's political, economic and social development" (301).

Composition of Malaysian Population

THE population of Malaysian citizens in 2018 was 29.1 million. The composition of Bumiputera ethnic groups accounted for 69.1% of total citizens. The composition of Chinese and Indians Department of Statistics Malaysia was 23.0% and 6.9%, respectively (Department of Statistics Malaysia, 2018). Malaysia is among many contemporary nations with a multiracial population including "fairly large minorities" (Smith 1981: 9). It is "one of the most delicately balanced multi racial societies" in Southeast Asia (Watson 19). In terms of population, Malaysia is a nation of indigenous races (Malays and aborigines) and immigrants (mostly Chinese, Indians and Eurasians) (Mohd. Taib 1973: 109). The Malays and the indigenous races are referred to as *bumiputera*, sons of the soil. There is a clear demarcation between the *bumiputera* and the *non-bumiputera* population, as the former's privileged position is enshrined in the Malaysian Constitution (Rao & Ross-Larson, 1977; Wan, 1983). This broad categorisation is further subdivided along racial or ethnic lines, as Malaysians are also identified according to essentialist labels (Hirschman 555). The term *bumiputera* can be traced back to the 1930s. It has become common usage since the 1970s with the increased preoccupation with Malay identity and the government's use of the term in its policies (Nagata 193).

Despite its mixed racial composition, Malaysia is perceived as a Malay country in Malay political thought (Rao & Ross-Larson 18).

This is largely because it is generally accepted that the Malays came to the Malay peninsula before the Chinese or Thais and it is therefore recognised as a Malay homeland (Provencher 103; Rao & Ross-Larson 17). The Malaysian Constitutional (Amendment) Act 1971 has further reinforced the situation. This Act forbids any discussion on such sensitive constitutional issues as the national language (Article 152), the special position of Malays (Article 153), the sovereignty of the Malay rulers (Article 181) and the whole question of citizenship rights (Section III).

The 13 May, 1969 Riots

THE 13 May 1969 riots have often been referred to Sino-Malay riots though it involved the other racial communities. The circumstances that led to this violence is closely linked to the celebratory rallies of the opposition parties after the 1969 general elections. There was a significant decline in the seats held by the government parties, the Alliance, from 89 to 67 seats in the Parliament. This resulted in a counter-rally by the Malays championed by United Malay National Organisation (UMNO) political leaders. The Malays felt threatened by this turn of events as they feared the position was being undermined. The violent clashes then erupted in the streets of Kuala Lumpur and in other major areas like Penang and Ipoh which resulted in loss of lives and property. A State of Emergency was declared and the Constitution was suspended (Andaya & Andaya 296-297).

The 13 May 1969 riots remain embedded in the Malaysian national psyche, a wound that is often reopened to create a sense of fear among the people. There was at least one major racial riot in 1967 and a few after the 1969 riots. Just over a year before the May 13 incident, there was a riot that had the whole nation at a standstill: The Penang Hartal Riot of 1967. The first day alone five were killed and ninety-two injured during the riot. When all was over, twenty-nine were dead, over two hundred hurt and around 1300 arrested.

Since the 13 May 1969 riots, there have been at the least two racial riots involving mainly Malays and Indians. First, the 1998

Penang racial riots where no deaths were reports and again in 2001, the Kampung Medan Riots, in the outskirts of Kuala Lumpur which was from 4th to 13th March, resulting in over four hundred people detained, over a hundred injured and six deaths.

The Voice of Doomsday Politicians:
The Threat of a Repeat of May 13, 1969

IT is becoming more common for Malay extremist nationalist groups to bandy the threat of a repeat of the 13 May 1969 riots whenever it suits them. These threats are often openly announced in public and widely published in the Malaysian media. These political groups and individual politicians have used the threat to Islam, Malay rights and the monarchy as the basis to threaten violence. For instance, a collective of groups from Malaysia's ethnic-Malay majority warned of a repeat in sectarian violence that rocked the country in the 1960s, amid escalating tensions with a minority Indian-based NGO that purportedly questioned the rights of Muslims. The group said it had formed a new front to defend Islam against "rude and dominant" groups from other races. They added: "Because the effect of this can bring about untoward threats and we are worried the dark history of May 13, 1969, would recur" (Yiswaree, 2017).

A prominent Malay politician Sharizat Abdul Jalil, at her party's general assembly warned that the May 13 tragedy might be repeated should UMNO become weak and unable to overcome its challenges (Koon, 2012). And yet another Malay politician, Jamal Yunos, well-known for his antics and controversial public (mis)behaviour announced in his Facebook: "I vow that the May 13 tragedy will be repeated and parang will fly if Bersih 5 is held at the same time, date and place as the #BERSIH5 rally scheduled on November 19. Long live the Malays!" ("IGP: Police Will Probe Jamal's Alleged May 13 Remarks", 2016). The Inspector-General of Police (IGP) Khalid Abu Bakar was reported in saying that the police will act against Red Shirts leader Jamal Yunos for allegedly threatening a repeat of the May 13 race riots.

A more recent threat of the repeat of the May 13, 1969 riots emerged when the government discussed ratifying the International Convention on the Elimination of All Forms of Racial Discrimination (ICERD). It was reported in the national media that Ahmad Farouk Musa, a Muslim activist said "This kind of sudden departure from the commitment was expected because it seems that right-wing Malay groups, especially like Gagasan Kuasa 3, were trying to incite racial hatred and bloodshed by invoking memories of the May 13 riots" ("No Choice but to Axe ICERD after Unrest Threats, Says Activist", 2018).

Illusions of Cultural Integration

FROM Independence till the riots in May 1969, there were no clear government policies or initiatives in terms of a national ideology to move the people in the direction of Malaysian nationalism. There was concern for national unity; the need for a sense of Malaysianness was articulated by Tan Siew Sin, a Cabinet Minister and the then President of the Malaysian Chinese Association:

> Before we can establish a really united nation, the major racial groups in the country must gradually come closer and closer together. The Malays must be less Malay in their outlook, the Chinese must be less Chinese, the Indians must be less Indian and so on, so that eventually we shall regard ourselves as Malaysian rather than as Malays, Chinese or Indians. (qtd. in Solehah 1)

Though the people were called upon to shed some of their cultural distinctiveness to consider themselves "Malaysians," little was said on what one had to acquire to achieve this and there was no clear idea of what was meant by the term "Malaysian culture" (Ratnam 136). In the late 1960s, at least two Malay(sian) leaders believed that they had succeeded in creating a "Malaysian" culture. First, the then Deputy Prime Minister Tun Abdul Razak, in 1967, indicated this when he proclaimed:

We have drawn from the richness of our multi racial heritage
and have built a Malaysian culture with an identity of its own.
We no longer speak of a Chinese, Indian or Malay culture. We
now speak of a Malaysian culture. (qtd. in Solehah 6)

Second, in April 1969, just a month before the violent racial riots
in Malaysia, Tuanku Abdul Rahman, the Prime Minister, expressed
his belief in the "fusion of the cultures of all our people into a
Malaysian cultural identity" (qtd. in Solehah 6). Both the leaders
were to be proved wrong. The 13 May 1969 riots revealed that "the
facade of multi racial co existence lasted until the by elections [*sic*]
of 1969 when sweeping Chinese victories threatened to upset Malay
political hegemony" (Solehah 7). It took Mahathir Mohamad to
acknowledge the actual state of affairs in Malaysia:

Looking back through the years, one of the startling facts
which must be admitted was that there was never true
racial harmony. There was a lack of inter racial strife.
There was tolerance. There was accommodation. But
there was no harmony. (Mahathir 1970: 4-5)

Mahathir Mohamad accurately sums up the pre 1969 Malaysian
situation. There was some accommodation but no integration as Tun
Abdul Razak and Tuanku Abdul Rahman had believed.

The Move Towards a National Culture

THE Malayan government from the time of independence
emphasized that "Malayan culture must be indigenously based"
(Wan 56). However, it was only after the May 1969 riots that the
basic characteristics of the nation began to be clearly defined. Malay
culture was to be the basis of national culture, the Malay rulers the
symbols of sovereignty, the Malay language the national language
and official language, and Islam the state religion (Wan 57).

Non-bumiputera Malaysians are led to believe that one way they could be assimilated into Malaysian society is through the acquiring of Malaysian national cultural identity. However, I believe that the Malay(sian) notion of a national Malaysian culture problematises the concept of being Malaysian.

The National Cultural Congress was instituted to clear up earlier ambiguities of what constituted Malaysian culture. Solehah Ishak presents the three main conclusions reached by the Congress:

> First, that the "principle that is used to shape national culture should be based on Malay culture." Second, since Islam was chosen as the "religion of the Federation," it was only natural that the National Cultural Congress should also make Islam an important element in the promotion of this "national identity." Third, to show that the other races have not been ignored, the Congress stipulated that the cultures of the Chinese and the Indians, where suitable and appropriate, "should be incorporated in the promulgation of a cultural identity," but the basic principle remains: Malaysian culture has to be based on the culture of the Malays. (Solehah 14)

This notion of Malaysian culture was reiterated by the then Prime Minister, Tun Abdul Razak, "Malaysian culture must be based on the culture of the indigenous people of this region. I want this to be properly understood so that there will be no more doubts or anxiety. It is important that we integrate suitable elements of culture and arts from the various cultures from this country [...]" (qtd. in Davies 209).

Solehah Ishak suggests that the Malaysian government's attempts at promoting Malaysian National Culture were a "juggling act [...] which can be read as accommodating the extremist Malays, moderate Malays and other Malaysians." She adds that, although good will among the races has been a concern, "the rules it is played by are Malay-based" (36).

Malaysian National Culture was not to develop as some like
Ryan rather naively believed: that a Malaysian culture would
evolve based on the civilisations of those people who make up
the population of the country, a culture which will be the result of
compromise, fusion and synthesis (Ryan xi). It was clearly to be
based and centred on Malay culture (Wan, 1983; Solehah, 1987).

Initiatives Towards a National Identity

AT the time when Malaysian National Culture was being engineered
(after the 13 May 1969 riots), the National Consultative Council was
set up to "establish positive and practical guidelines for inter racial
cooperation and social integration" (Milne 573). This Council worked
out the new national ideology, or the Rukun Negara. It was designed to
ensure acceptance of the existing Constitution and also promote nation
building and overcome existing primordial loyalties (Milne 573).

In July 1969, Tan Sri Ghazali Shafie announced that Malaysia
was to have a national ideology, suggesting a new approach to the
ethnic problems in the country (Milne 563). The national ideology
was called the Rukun Negara. Besides being aimed at integrating
and uniting the people, it was to be used as a means to strengthen the
political status quo. The five principles of the Rukun Negara are:

> Belief in God
> Loyalty to King and Country
> Upholding the Constitution
> Rule of Law
> Good Behaviour and Morality (Wan 90)

The Rukun Negara as an ideology was intended to serve as
a means to bind the different racial groups in Malaysia and help
individual citizens integrate into Malaysian society. As an ideology,
it was to help in "domesticating primordialism" and serve the Malay-
dominated government as a means of achieving political consensus
and legitimising its authority. More importantly, it was to help

establish Malay political hegemony in the country. Its implementation also categorically destroyed all hopes of *non-bumiputera* Malaysians who preferred cultural pluralism to assimilation into the dominant Malay culture of establishing a Malaysian Malaysia (Wan 73-94).

In accepting this ideology, non Malays were submitting to the legitimacy of the Malay regime (Milne 567). The government's policy towards national unity was generally viewed as a means of destroying the distinct cultural elements of the immigrant communities and replacing them with something which is distinctly Malaysian (McGee, 1964; Selvaratnam, 1974; Wan, 1983).

Malaysian playwright, Kee Thuan Chye, succinctly presents Malaysian life after the 13 May 1969 riots to Mohammad A. Quayum in an interview:

> [Before the riots] we had lived together harmoniously [...] There had been no sign of antagonism. Of course, the factor of "Otherness" was there in our interactions but we were familiar with each other [...] We never felt, "Ugh, he's Malay (or Chinese or Indian) so better not have anything to do with him." We played together, we laughed together [...] we had no idea that the [event] would radically change the whole pattern of life in the country and negatively intensify the idea of "Otherness" in all of us. To this day, relations between Malays and non-Malays have never been the same.
>
> (Mohammad A. Quayum 2005: 135)

Kee's statements reveal the divided nation that Malaysia had become as a result of the May 13, 1969 riots and also the challenges lay ahead for Bangsa Malaysia or Malaysian race to become a reality.

Representation of May 13, 1969 Riots in Malaysian Literature in English

MALAYSIAN literature in English, a legacy of British colonialism, and emerging in the 1940s, is very much a product of the English education system (both at school and university levels). The Malaysian writer in English is a late arrival in a nation with a long classical literary tradition in the Malay language which dates back to the 15th century (Mohd. Taib 1986: 19) and a fast-developing modern Malay literary tradition which is said to have begun in the 18th century (Mohd. Taib 1986: 21). As such, the presence of the Malaysian writer in English has not been not greeted with great enthusiasm.

The Malaysian political agenda openly places Malaysian writers writing in English outside the mainstream Malaysian society as writing in a language which is not considered part of the national literary tradition. Brewster's comment on the dilemma of writing in a colonial language applies accurately to Malaysian writers using English as their literary medium. She states, "Just as the colonized writer is ironically aware of his hegemonic marginalization in the colonial context, so post colonial writers are aware of the hegemony of nationalism" (142).

In relation to this, Simms also posits that in Malaysia,

> insofar as the government speaks for the nation, English is an intrusion to be tolerated only in the most private and domestic situations, a threat not merely of past colonial sensibilities but an overt challenge by the mercantile community of Chinese and sometimes Indian minorities; and so for the English poet (this will include all writers in English) in Malaysia his language alienates him from the public life and from the spiritual richness of the community as a whole. (9)

Despite the uncongenial environment for writing in English the number of Malaysians writing in English has been on the rise. And these Malaysian writers who write in English are very aware of the restrictions placed on all writers in this country. Malaysian writer, K.S. Maniam is acutely aware of the restrictions placed upon a writer. In an interview in 1986, Kee expresses his concern, which is representative for all Malaysian writers:

We can't describe things as openly as we want to. There are so many subjects here that are called "sensitive issues." In literature, these sensitive issues make a bigger list than in politics. And you also can't describe personal obsessions or personal fantasies which have to do with sex unless you sugar-coat it. (1992: 15)

Maniam reiterates his concern for the restrictions imposed on him, as a writer, which often conflict with his desire to write honestly. He states:

The underlying implication is that there are issues that cannot be approached directly so as not to offend any community or authority. (171)

Kee Thuan Chye, a Malaysian, expresses similar concerns as Maniam. He states:

a writer must write with the courage of his conviction. He must brook no compromise and he must not fear the consequence. He must be prepared to sacrifice his own comfort and safety if it is demanded of him. (2001: 67)

Kee says this fully aware of the Malaysian stringent censorship laws. Salleh ben Joned is one of the better-known Malaysian writers, who attempts to test the limits of these laws and criticises the writers who practice self-censorship either consciously or unconsciously. He states:

If self-censorship is bad for the general intellectual development of the country, it's worse for the development of its literature [...] But as it involves creative writers, this self-censorship can be so ingrained in certain areas of thinking and feeling (that involve religion, say or race) that it no longer appears like self-

censorship. It operates at the level of the unconcious,
even before the imagination can produce the germ of an
idea or perception. (Salleh 52-53)

Ee Tiang Hong captures these restrictions and the forced self-
censorship writers and the general public have to adhere to in his
poem, "Nospeak" (1978):

In that (unmentionable) country
it's against the law to speak
about certain things.
Everyone is free, however,
to suggest ways and means
to improve these very things,
subject to only one condition—
no one shall question
the status of these things,
which are sacred that's why
it's against the law
to speak against the things. (1985: 10)

Lee Joo For's Dark Humour in the Treatment of Cross-Cultural Violence

LEE Joo For's play "The Happening in the Bungalow" was written
in 1969 and performed in 1970. It was written in the year of the
May 13 riots. Though the main focus of the play revolves around the
main character Birch, a fictional descendent of the British Resident
murdered in Perak in 1875. The plot revolves around Birch's revenge
for the murder of his ancestor, by attempting to rape his Malay secretary,
Rozni. Humour runs through the play until towards the end with the
mention of crowd violence and killings, none of it on stage, except
for Birch accidentally shooting and killing his Malay servant, Boy.

In "The Happening in the Bungalow," Lee Joo For draws from
two historical moments from Malaysian history. First, the killing of a

British Resident in 1875 which led to the British intervention to the Malay states and second, the 13 May 1969 riots. The May 13 riots is a significant backdrop for this play. Birch's servant, Boy, describes the commotion he had witnessed and has run back to the bungalow:

> BOY: You know, Che' Rozni, there's plenty of trouble outside in the kampungs, villages and streets […] I see some and hear some. People fighting people, people killing people, people burning houses, police coming and shooting, soldiers coming and shooting, then the police and soldiers go away and then people come out and fight again. (Lee 140)

On discovering that he had unintentionally shot and killed Boy, Birch walks out into the violent crowd, carrying the dead Boy. The stage directions indicate that the crowd sets upon Birch and kill him. The play has a rather ambivalent ending. Outside, the people are shouting:

> OUTSIDE VOICES:
> (1) Kill-kill-kill the other kind of people!
> (2) Fight back! Kill the others! Blood for blood! Kill! Kill! Kill!

But on stage:

> ROZNI: Cheng, I'm going to break a custom. I'm going to tell you—with all my heart I love you!
> [They embrace again.]   (Lee 143)

The ending of the play with the violence outside is contrasted with the love scene between a Malay and Chinese character inside, on stage. The audience are left to ponder on the May riots which are still fresh in their minds. Of Lee's treatment of the race riots, Fernando states: "The humour serves as a balm over a more serious problem of culture-conflict hinted at by the play, but which Lee, however, has not the resources to cope with it yet" (Fernando 1972: xv).

The Burden and Disillusionment of Malaysian Nation in Ee Tiang Hong's Poems

THE next two works discussed are poems by Ee Tiang Hong published in 1976 and in 1985. Ee left Malaysia and went on a self-exile in 1975. He became an Australian and lived in there till his death in 1990. The turn of events in Malaysia from 13 May 1969 weighed heavily upon him. Kirpal Singh describes Ee's poetry:

> [a] manifest testimony to the burden he carried—both external and, more significantly, internal. Much of what he articulates in his poems about history, especially the convoluted history of Malaya becoming Malaysia and becoming a nation, is uncomfortable. The trauma of internalised realisation of what history was doing to his beloved country, how history was unfolding before his very eyes, how, indeed, history was being made and manufactured (that is, how history was being distorted/ modified/communicated en masse/altered/edited) so as to fit the times and the morals, as he ruefully put it in one of his poems. (25)

Two of Ee's poems, "Kuala Lumpur, May 1969" (1985) and "Requiem" (1976) make direct reference to the violence and impact of 13 May 1969 riots on Malaysians. In 'Kuala Lumpur, May 1969' the persona narrates how the family counted itself lucky away from the violence and safe. In the second stanza, there is mentioned how the government-controlled media presents the incident:

> On black-and-white tv
> spasmodic national bulletins.
> discrete shots of charred wreckage,

soldiers in leopard-spot uniform, barbed barricade,
ministerial explanations of the causes of the riots,
reasons for the curfew. (1985: 29)

The final stanza in the poem brings out the poet's sense of sorrow and loss with the passing of time:

As now more and more distant,
bitterness, recrimination day by day subside,
ashes on flower, leaf and shoot
in the sparse valley of a memory. (1985: 29)

Ee's prayerful poem "Requiem" recalls the catastrophic event. The survivors now have a choice to remember the "the lessons of May 13" or forget the deaths of their loved ones:

Tell your children to remember
The lessons of May 13,
Or tell them to forget
The friends or relatives who died,
It makes no difference,
Sun and moon will rise tomorrow
Sun and moon will set
For all our sorrows. (1976: 55)

Twenty-five years after the May 13 riots, in 1994, Ee's disillusionment with Malaysia's continued preoccupation with race, language, religion and birthplace is evident in his poem, "Some New Perspectives"(1994):

Race, language, religion, birthplace—
the categories do not satisfy:
what do they say of you and me.
the space, the silences between? (1994: 10)

The country has not moved forward and Ee wants it to be recognised that these are failed concepts and in the last two lines of the poem Ee calls for something more inclusive:

> a world view,
> the twentieth century's, ours (1994: 10).

Ee's poems address directly the issues of race, belonging and moving beyond the race. These are sad poems and they also raise questions Malaysian need to address to come to terms, the choose to accept and stay or like him find them unacceptable and leave.

The Failure of Social Engineering:
Ghulam Sarwar Yousuf's "May 13, 1969"

ANOTHER poet, Ghulam Sarwar Yousuf, in his poem "May 13, 1969" (1982) addresses the government's failed attempt to bring a cohesiveness in Malaysian society:

> the surgical expedient
> of a decade or more
> though hopeful apparently
> was no skin-graft
> or socio-cultural
> alchemy (34)

He recognises that social engineering did not work, but is hopeful that the society will heal and recover from this calamity:

> but the flesh will heal
> in its own good time
> souls will graft
> their own curious way. (34)

Ghulam Sarwar Yousuf's concerns about a unified Malaysian society resonates which what Homi Bhabha describes as containment in cultural diversity. Malaysia's attempt at bringing together the different races reflects what Homi Bhabha posits:

> A transparent norm is constituted, a norm given by the host society or dominant culture, which says that these other cultures are fine, but we must be able to locate them within our own grid. (208)

Bhabha, too, acknowledges that "it is actually very difficult, even impossible and counterproductive, to try and fit together different forms of culture and to pretend that they can easily coexist" (209). He, however, goes on to assert that

> all forms of culture are continually in a process of hybridity. But for me the importance of hybridity is not to be able to trace two original moments from which the third space emerges, rather hybridity to me is the "third space" which enables other positions to emerge. This third space displaces the histories that constitute it and sets up a new structure of authority, new political initiatives, which are inadequately understood through received wisdom. (211)

Bhabha's notion of the "third space" can be linked with the Malay(sian) notion of a national culture. However, there is only one common point. Both recognise the merging of cultures into a hybrid culture. There are contrasting views on the means of achieving this hybrid culture and how the results of the merging are to be perceived.

Bhabha perceives the process of hybridity as a consequence of the merging of cultures, unengineered or planned. The importance of this hybridity lies "in not to be able to trace two original moments" (211). Bhabha's sense of a hybrid culture seems an idealized form, where the original cultures remain untraceable. In reality, no matter how tightly cultures become interwoven and distilled, their roots are rarely completely obliterated. The Malay(sian) attempts at national unity, on the other hand, is both deliberate and planned. It is a conscious attempt to create a national culture which continues to give importance to the original culture from which it had been grafted.

As such, and as indicated by Solehah Ishak (1987), Malaysian culture remains very much Malay culture and contrasts with Bhabha's notion of the process of hybridity which should result in "something different, something new and unrecognisable, a new area of negotiation of meaning and representation" (Bhabha 211). The very nature of cultural engineering in Malaysia is to give continued pre-eminence to Malay culture in the hybrid Malaysian culture.

Malaysian Novelists' Treatment of May 13, 1969 Riots

IT is an interesting point to note that prose writers discussed in this paper with regards to the portrayal of the May 13, 1969 riots, be it of novels, short stories, or plays, the protagonists are from the same race as the writers, the only exception being Lloyd Fernando, whose main characters are primarily Malays. In Lloyd Fernando's novel, *Green is the Colour* (1993), Dahlan and Sara are the main characters with Yun Min a Chinese character.

Green is the Colour deals with the violence and its aftermath on characters from different ethnic groups. It begins immediately after the violent riots in a tensed atmosphere: "Everybody spoke a different language, everybody used different words, everyone was hurt and angry that the others did not understand them" (Fernando 1993: 59). Sara's thoughts on 13 May 1969 are presented as follows:

> Nobody could get May sixty-nine right, she thought. It was hopeless to pretend you could be objective about it. Speaking even to someone close to you, you were careful for fear the person might unwittingly quote you to others. If a third person was present, it was worse, you spoke for that person's benefit. If he was Malay you spoke one way,

Chinese another way, Indian another. Even if he wasn't
listening. In the end the spun tissue, like an unsightly
scab, become your vision of what happened: the wound
beneath continued to run pus. (Fernando 1993: 93)

Mohammad A. Quayum states that Fernando uses this dystopian
environment after the riots "to embark on his soul-searching process
for the nation: how could this dreadful ordeal be overcome and
peace be found in the future, or how could the country attain unity
and homogeneity in spite of its racial and cultural diversity?" (2007:
73-74). Different characters have their own vision of Malaysia.
Panglima's is a Malay Malaysia while Omar's is an Islamic
Malaysia. Siti Sarah, Dahlan and Yun Ming have an inclusive vision
of Malaysia, which includes all the different races. Yun Ming is of
the view that Malaysians should "understand one another" (Fernando
1993: 69) and he refuses to go to either his wife and child in England
or with his brother in Australia.

Shirley Geok-lin Lim's *Joss and Gold* (2001) is set about a year
before the riots till the day of the riots and spans a period of thirteen
years. The novel presents Malaysian life on a broader canvas, set
in three places, Kuala Lumpur, New York and Singapore, from
1968 to 1981, and how the May 13, 1969 riots continue to haunt its
characters. The characters in novel can be seen in two racial camps,
the Malay and non-Malays (Indian and Chinese). In Book 1 of *Joss
and Gold* Lim presents the conflicting views held by these characters.
The May 13, 1969 riots seem raw and the races are still divided. The
Malay characters, Abdullah and Samad, see Li An, Ellen, and Gina as
"other" because of their ethnic differences. For Abdullah and Samad,
Malaysia is the country of the Malays and if anyone disputes that
view, they "should be imprisoned or sent back to China or India" (Lim
78). Abdullah expects the other races to assimilate into Malay culture:
"We need a single set of values to keep us together" (Lim 182).

Li An, on the other hand, believes in Bangsa Malaysia.
Unlike Abdullah and Samad, she believes Indians and Chinese are
Malaysians. She wants a more inclusive Malaysia where the different

races co-exist in equality. For Li An, "[e]verything in Malaysia is champor-champor, mixed, rojak. A little Malay, a little Chinese, a little Indian, a little English. Malaysian means rojak, and if mixed right, it will be delicious" (Lim 45). She goes on to add: "Give us a few more years and we'll be a totally new nation. No more Malay, Chinese, Indian, but all one people" (Lim 45).

Li An goes to the extent of rejecting her own Chinese identity and affirms in a conversation with her husband, "I am not Chinese. I'm Malaysian" (Lim 71). Later she writes in her diary: "All this talk about Chinese rights makes me sick too. Malay rights, Chinese rights. No one talks about Malaysian rights. I am a Malaysian. I don't exist" (Lim 90).

As in the case of the characters in Fernando's novel *Green is the Colour*, in Lim's *Joss and Gold* we see characters holding opposing views about a shared Malaysia. Those holding a more inclusive Malaysia will have to contend with those who see a Malay Malaysia.

In Preeta Samarasan's novel, *Evening is the Whole Day* (2008), the May 13, 1969 riots are seen through the lived experience of a Malaysian Indian family. The novel begins in September 6, 1980 and closes on August 29, 1980. Between these dates, the novel moves in a series of flashbacks, the May 13, 1969 riots are given a full chapter entitled, "Power Struggles" (Samarasan 110-135). The immediacy of the riots is captured in the novel as the characters get caught up in the actual events. Samarasan's treatment of the riots is both stylised and matter of fact in its portrayal. Samarasan presents the imagined threat and fear among the races as a fatal dance between "Rumor" and "Fact" which then erupted into violence and mayhem on the streets of Kuala Lumpur:

> Impossible to say, but three days after the election, Rumor and Fact burst forth into noonday Kuala Lumpur heat, Rumor in a red dress, Fact in coat and tails, and together they began a salacious tango in the streets.
>
> (Samarasan 120)

In the following paragraph the narrator asks:

> Was it Rumour or Fact that ragged crowds of Indians
> and Chinese had trailed through Malay settlements with
> promises and suggestions? *Your turn to lick our boots!*
> *Talk about ketuanan Malayu, now we'll see who's tuan!*
> *Kuala Lumpur belongs the Chinese. Balek Kampung!*
> *Go back to your backwater villages.* Go home. Go back
> where you came from. (Samarasan 121)

Samarasan follows this up by presenting a Malaysian Pandora
clad in a sarong donning a hibiscus behind her ear, the national
flower of the country, to open her box releasing the complications of
Malaysian racial strife:

> These words fluttered blackly out, and in no time it
> ceased to matter whether they had really been spoken
> or not. They were real and here to stay. They burst into
> flames; they blazed plain in view and brought tears to
> unprotected eyes. Anyone could say those words now.
> A could spit them to B, B to C, and C could turn around
> and spit them back to A. Because really, in this country,
> that go home cry could be directed—delicately or not so
> delicately—at just about anyone. (Samarasan 121-122)

This "go home" call hurled at Indians and Chinese continues to
be a contentious issue in Malaysia. In Bernice Chauly's poem "Still"
there is now a desire for the call to be hurled back at the Malays:

> And where will this take us?
> It is easy to burn pictures
> It is easy to torch churches
> It is easy to say "Allah is for us"
> It is easy to say "Go home, back to India"
> […]

We want to say "Babi, you go home"
We want to say "What is Malay?"
We want to say "What is Malaysian?" (7)

The poem highlights the problem of belonging and identity, for Malaysians. The "us" in line 1 could refer to all the races or the other races besides the Malay while "we" in the three lines certainly excludes the Malay. The notion of the Other remains unresolved even after forty-four years, when this poem was published, and it still remains fifty years on at the time of writing this paper.

The most recent novel examined in this paper is a young adult novel by Hanna Alkaf, entitled, *The Weight of Our Sky* (2019). In an interview with Terence Toh (2019), published in a Malaysian English language national newspaper, Hanna Alkaf says the following are the reasons why she wrote this young adult now:

> I had always been fascinated by the May 13 riots. We know they happened, and we're threatened by the spectre of it every once in a while by some politician. But we never really hear about what actually happened.
>
> In our textbooks, it's just a couple of paragraphs, and it's really sterile. I wanted to know what it felt like, what people actually went through," says the KL-born author.
>
> I had never seen it (May 13) reflected in our literature, especially literature targeted at young people.
>
> And I was worried that, even in my generation, we don't really know about it. The further we get away from it, the less that young people know, and the less people will remember it.
>
> If we gloss over the worst parts of our history and we don't make an effort to preserve it, we run the risk of repeating it. We have to learn from it. (Toh, 2019)

Hanna Alkaf raises most of the issues that continue to plague Malaysian society about the May 13, 1969 riots. She highlights how little is really known by Malaysian on the riots and how it is still used by politicians to intimidate Malaysians.

This young adult novel, *The Weight of Our Sky*, has appeared on the Malaysian literary landscape at an appropriate time, fifty years after the riots, when the May 13, 1969 riots still looms as a backdrop to scare Malaysians into submitting into racist politicians' agendas. Though the characters in this novel are caught up in the violence of the riots, this is presented without any gore. Melati witnesses her best friend, Safiyah, being taken away from her for being a Malay and her death seems inevitable at the hands of the Chinese mob and is finally confirmed at the end of the novel. Melati escapes a similar fate, having been rescued by a Chinese woman who says that Melati is a Eurasian. The death of her friend then becomes a guilt she has to bear, for being alive while Safiyah had died.

Despite the instances of racial strife, the attempts to provide help by characters of the different races to one another gives hope for a nation struggling to find a way to co-exist in harmony. The number of people killed at the end of the riots remains unclear. The figures released by the government is in doubt.

Melati's mother, a nurse who works in the government hospital says, "I saw the bodies with my own eyes" and adds "No way there were only one hundred ninety-six, No way. She was referring to the government report that only 196 had been killed during the riots. Her observation receives this response: "Must save face mah," Uncle Chong, said quietly" (Hanna 274-275).

The four novelists discussed in this paper, have examined the portrayal of violent riots that shook the very core of the nation in 1969. These novels were published from 1993 to 2019, the first appearing 26 years after the riots and the latest on the 50th anniversary of the riots. The writers comprise, two Indians, a Chinese and a Malay. Their characters all grapple with what it means to be Malaysian. Race and religion appear as major obstacles and struggles for the characters to move forward towards a unified and peaceful nation. The novelists have no easy solution to offer though some of their characters want a more inclusive Malaysia with equality for all.

Malay Guilt and the May 13, 1969 Riots

THE treatment of the 13 May 1969 riots by two Malay writers presents an interesting phenomenon of guilt in the protagonists in a short story and in a play. In Karim Raslan's short story, "Heroes" (1997), a daughter harasses her aging seventy-eight year old father to reveal the truth about the handicapped Nazrin, a man, she has seen coming to their home in a taxi and her father giving him money. She insists:

> I want to know about that boy—Nazrin. He used to visit the house all the time in those days. I want to why you were so kind to him. Mak used to say you were very courageous and brave in those months. (Karim 27)

Fariza, the daughter, then asks her father to write about the past as he seems unable to speak about it, and he reluctantly agrees to do so. Karim Raslan presents the father's thoughts on what his daughter wants to know, informing the reader about the father's view on the May 13, 1969 riots:

> When she says "the past," I know what she really means. She wants me to write an account of May '69—as if the events of those bloody weeks explain the decades that followed. I've been trying to tell her the past isn't just '69. 1969 is an aberration, a ghastly aberration and nothing more. (Karim 30)

In his last journal entry, Fariza's father describes the role he had played as an important and faithful government servant, having to work with other political parties. His work required him to travel the Peninsula, for the "preservation of the Malay race" (Karim 33).

An incident while on the road involving Nazrin becomes a dark secret her father has had to carry for the rest of his life. The car that the father was travelling in hits a Chinese woman and they are soon set upon by a Chinese mob, reminding Fariza's father of what had happened in Chow Kit and Kampung Baru. Completely overwhelmed by his fear for their lives, he instructs the driver to leave the scene of the accident, his mission still in the forefront of his mind. Nazrin, his young assistant, is nowhere near them and is abandoned to his fate. The father is full of remorse for his actions:

> Had I, in releasing the handbrake, been responsible for it all, for Nazrin's terrible injuries, his crippled state, my fears, and my disgrace?

> I had witnessed my own 'fall': lived through it. I had seen myself at my worst. Nothing I could ever do, would match this failure. (Karim 47)

Fariza, meanwhile finds Nazrin and discovers the truth for herself. Nazrin does not blame her father for his injury. Still, Fariza blames her father, "What happened? Ayah, you're my hero. You let me down" (Karim 36).

The discovery of the truth tears them apart and he says to her: "Fariza, the truth isn't always worth knowing" (Karim 36). Despite what he says to his daughter, he is still haunted by the past and his cowardice of which he laments: "We ran like dogs with our tails between our legs" (Karim 49).

In Jit Murad's play *Spilt Gravy on Rice* (first copyright in 2002, revised in 2003, and published in 2017) one of the issues that another Malay father deals with is his own demon which is also linked to May 13, 1969 riots. There are a few references to the riots and a young man, Nordin, the father had brought into their household in this play. In Scene 10 of the play, one of the siblings, Zakaria brings up Nordin's name to Kalsom and his involvement in the violence of the 13 May riots:

Zakaria: Som, Do you remember Nordin? Wonder what happened to him? Bapak's adopted son?

Kalsom: Wasn't like that. He was the driver. [...] Bapak felt responsible for him. You always feel responsible for the orang kampung in your household.

Zakaria: Whatever. Do you remember anything of May 13?

Kalsom: (freezes a bit) I was a kid, but I remember the, uh, tension at home.

Zakaria: Remember when Nordin came back late one night?

Kalsom: Stop, Zak.

Zakaria: He said he and his "uniformed friends" had set up a roadblock on the Federal Highway, stopping cars all day.

Kalsom: What're you doing, you bastard? Nobody wants to hear this!

Zakaria: Remember how his eyes were wild and he couldn't stop laughing? Like he didn't notice that he was drenched in blood. (Jit 347)

Nordin's laughter can be linked to the hysteria of the violence he had committed. Nordin, as seen through the eyes of Bapak, was a kampung boy was not quite ready for the city. This explains Nordin being led by the city boys and his involvement in the violence on the Federal Highway. Bapak had also misjudged Nordin, entrusting the family to him and also the household matters. Bapak sees Nordin's betrayal when he finds out that Zakaria had been sexually abused by Nordin, something Zaitun had also discovered. Still, Nordin wasn't sent away but allowed to remain as the family's driver. Nordin, Bapak's failed portege, was violently involved in the May 13 riots and he had sexually abused Zakaria but Bapak's guilt makes it impossible for him to sever his bonds with the miscreant.

Both Karim Raslan and Jit Murad explore the complexities of responsibility and betrayal experienced by their Malay characters, during the 13 May riots. Their personal lives are forever changed either by their own actions or those they had trusted.

May 13, 1969 Riots: A Memory

OVER time, the 13 May 1969 riots become a moment in Malaysian history, a part of an individual's memory of a violent event in the past. Two Malaysian writers give evidence of this. Paul Ganaselvam, in his short story, "A Journey's End" (2013), gives a single line reference to the May 13, 1969 riots. The story revolves around the life of Queen Mary, a young 17-year-old Indian bride, who leaves her homeland in 1939. The story spans over thirty years to 1970. Towards the end of the story, the narrator highlights the landmark events of Queen Mary and her husband's lives and how they had survived it all, "the invading Japanese, and the racial riots on [*sic*] May 1969" (Gnanaselvam 21).

A similar treatment of the May 13, 1969 riots is seen in Malachi Edwin Vethamani's poem, "Still Brickfields" (2016). The poet examines the gentrification of an area known as Brickfields in Kuala Lumpur. The persona in the poem bemoans how various events had contributed to the loss of his home and village. The May riots was one of these events:

> The river bank is concrete
> the lalang and weeds gone.
> The river wears
> a monsoon drain mask.
>
> There I once caught fish
> and saw floating corpses
> during the May riots
> that undid us. (40)

The "corpses" refer to the victims of the May 13 riots whose bodies floated down the Klang river. In this poem, the riots become one of the many events that have brought about changes to the villages in Brickfields. It is treated in a matter of fact manner, another event in the history of Malaysia and how it impinges on the lives of ordinary people.

Conclusion

MALAYSIAN writers in the English language address many issues and events that are important to Malaysia, though their presence continues to be marginalised in the country. The May 13, 1969 riots has been the subject of the works of many of these writers. It continues to remain a violent historical moment, a wound with a visible scar that is still seen and felt after fifty years. It is often hung around the necks of Malaysians like an albatross, a curse that will weigh heavy on the people, as its recurrence is often reiterated by unscrupulous politicians. The Malaysian writers, however, have treated this event with caution and sensitivity, not because of the censorship laws but because they write to come to terms with it and to see ways forward for the nation to heal from this wound.

WORKS CITED

Ahmad, Aijaz (1992) *In Theory* (London: Verso).

Andaya, B.W. & L.Y. Andaya (2001) *A History of Malaysia*. 2nd ed. (Basingstoke: Palgrave).

Bhabha, Homi K. (1990) "The Third Space: Interview with Homi Bhabha." Jonathan Rutherford (ed.): *Identity, Communnity, Culture, Difference* (London: Lawrence and Wishart), 207-221.

Brewster, Anne (1987) "The Discourse of Nationalism and Multiculturalism in Singapore and Malaysia in the 1950s and 1960s." *SPAN*, no.24: 136-150.

Chauly, Bernice (2013) *Onkalo* (Singapore: Math Paper Press).

Davies, Derek (ed.) (1974) *Far Eastern Economic Review Asia, 1974 Year Book* (Hong Kong: Far Eastern Econimic Review Ltd).

Department of Statistics Malaysia (2018) "Current Population Estimate, Malaysia, 2017-2018." Department of Statistics Malaysia (www.dosm.gov.my).

Ee Tiang Hong (1976) *Myths for the Wilderness* (Singapore: Heinemann Asia).

Ee Tiang Hong (1985) *Tranquerah* (Singapore: National University of Singapore Press).

Ee Tiang Hong (1994) *Nearing a Horizon* (Singapore: Unipress).

Fernando, Lloyd (1993) *Green Is the Colour* (Singapore: Landmark Publishers).

Fernando, Lloyd (ed.) (1972) *New Drama One* (Singapore: Oxford University Press).

Ghulam Sarwar Yousuf (1982) *Perfumed Memories* (Singapore: Graham Brash).

Gnanaselvam, Paul (2013) *Latha's Christmas and Other Stories* (Petaling Jaya: MPH Group Publishing).

Hanna Alkaf (2019) *The Weight of Our Sky* (New York: Salaam Reads, Simon & Schuster).

Hirschman, Charles (1987) "The Meaning and Mesasurement of Ethnicity in Malaysia: An Analysis of Census Classification." *The Journal of Asian Studies* 43.3: 555-582.

"IGP: Police Will Probe Jamal's Alleged May 13 Remarks"(2016). *Malay Mail*, 9 Oct. (www.malaymail.com/news/malaysia/2016/10/09/igp-police-will-probe-jamals-alleged-may-13-remarks/1224087).

Jit Murad (2017) *Plays* (Petaling Jaya: Matahari Books).

Karim Raslan (1997) *Heroes and Other Stories* (Singapore: Times Books International).

Kee Thuan Chye (1992) *Just in So Many Words: Views, Reviews & Other Things* (Singapore: Heinemann Asia).

Kee Thuan Chye (2001) "Dilemma of a Dog Barking at a Mountain: Pragmatist-Idealist Dialectic and the Writer in Malaysia." Mohammad A. Quayum & Peter C. Wicks (eds.): *Malaysian Literature in English: A Critical Reader* (Petaling Jaya: Pearson Education Malaysia), 67-72.

Kirpal Singh (2009) "Poetry and the Politics of History: Revisiting Ee Tiang Hong." *Asiatic* 3.2: 25-37.

Koon Yew Yin (2012) "A Gulf of 44 Years Separates Us from 13 May 1969." *Centre on Policy Initiatives*, 7 Dec. (www.cpiasia.net/v3/index.php/211-Columnists/koon-yew-yin/2449-a-gulf-of-44-years-separates-us-from-13-may-1969).

Lee Joo For (1972) "A Happening in the Bungalow." Fernando (ed.) 1972: 107-144.

Lim, Shirley Geok-lin (2001) *Joss and Gold* (Singapore: Times

Books International).

Mahathir Mohamad (1970) *The Malay Dilemma* (Singapore: Donald Moore for Asia Pacific Press).

Mahathir Mohamad (1992) *Malaysia: The Way Forward (Vision 2020)* (Kuala Lumpur: Malaysian Business Council).

Maniam, K.S. (1988) "The Malaysian Novelist: Detachment and Spiritual Transcendence." Bruce Bennett, et al. (eds.): *A Sense of Exile* (Nedlands: The Centre for Studies in Australian Literature, The University of Western Australia), 167-172.

McGee, T.G. (1964) "Population: A Preliminary Analysis." Wang Gungwu (ed.): *Malaysia: A Survey* (London: Pall Mall Press), 67-75.

Milne, R.S. (1970) "National Ideology and Natio Building in Malaysia." *Asian Survey* 10.7: 563-573.

Mohammad A. Quayum (2005) "Confessions of a Liminal Writer: An Interview with Kee Thuan Chye." *Kunapipi* 17.1: 130-139.

Mohammad A. Quayum (2007) "'My Country'/'Our Country': Race Dynamics and Contesting Nationalisms in Lloyd Fernando's *Green Is the Colour* and Shirley Geok-lin Lim's *Joss and Gold*." *Crossroads: An Interdisciplinary Journal of Southeast Asian Studies* 18.2: 65-89.

Mohd. Taib Osman (1973) "Towards the Development of Malaysia's National Literature." *Tenggara*, no.6: 105-120.

Mohd. Taib Osman (1986) *The Development of Malay Literature* (Kuala Lumpur: Times Books International).

Nagata, Judith A. (1984) *The Reflowering of Malaysian Islam* (Vancouver: University of British Columbia).

"No Choice but to Axe ICERD after Unrest Threats, Says Activist" (2018). *Free Malaysia Today*, 23 Nov. (www.freemalaysiatoday.com/category/nation/2018/11/23/putrajaya-right-in-axing-icerd-ratification-says-intellectual/).

Provencher, Ronald (1987) "Interethnic Conflict in the Malay Peninsular." Jerry Boucher, Daniel R. Landis & Karen Arnold Clark (eds.): *Ethnic Perspectives* (London: Sage Publications), 92-118.

Rao, Chandriah Appa & Bruce Ross-Larson (eds.) (1977) *Issues in Contemporary Malaysia* (Kuala Lumpur: Heinnemann Educational Books).

Ratnam, K.J. (1965) *Communalism and the Political Process in Malaysia* (Kuala Lumpur: University of Malaya Press).

Ryan, N.J. (1971) *The Cultural Heritage of Malay* (Kuala Lumpur: Longman Malaysia).

Salleh ben Joned (1994) *As I Please: Selected Writings 1975-1994* (London: Skoob Books).

Samarasan, Preeta (2008) *Evening Is the Whole Day* (London: Harper Collins Publishers).

Selvaratnam, S.V. (1974) *Decolonization, the Ruling Elite and Ethnic Relations in Peninsular Malaysia* (Brighton: Institute of Development Studies, University of Sussex).

Simms, Norman (1980) "The Future of English as a Poetic Medium in Singapore and Malaysia Part Three." *Quarterly World Report* 3.2: 8-12.

Smith, Anthony D. (1981) *The Ethnic Revival* (Cambridge: Cambridge University Press).

Solehah Ishak (1987) *Histrionics of Development: A Study of Three Contemporary Malay Playwrights* (Kuala Lumpur: Dewan Bahasa dan Pustaka).

Toh, Terence (2019) "Hanna Alkaf Dives into Racial Riots, Mental Health on Debut YA Novel." *The Star*, 13 Mar. (www.thestar. com.my/lifestyle/people/2019/03/13/hanna-alkaf-debut-novel).

Vethamani, Malachi Edwin (2018) *Complicated Lives* (Petaling Jaya: Maya Press).

Wan Hashim (1983) *Race Relations in Malaysia* (Kuala Lumpur: Heinemann Educational Books).

Watson, Keith (1979) "Education Policies in Multi-Cultural Societies." *Comparative Education* 15.1: 17-31.

Yiswaree Palansamy (2017) "Malay Groups Band Together to Fight Those Who Are Anti-Islam, Warn of May 13 Reoccurence." *Malay Mail*, 26 Apr. (www.malaymail.com/news/malaysia/ 2017/04/26/malay-groups-band-together-to-fight-those-who-are-anti-islam-warn-of-may-13/1364581).

Post-trauma
A Comparison of the Malay and Chinese Psyches in Response to the May 13 Tragedy in Their Literary Works from 1969 to 2019

Florence KUEK

I. Introduction

THE memory of the May 13, 1969 tragedy still haunts Malaysian society decades after its occurrence. As the incident marks one of the most severe sectarian violence between the Malay and Chinese thus far, May 13 has unfailingly been used by Malaysia's former ruling government as its trump card to defy opposing powers and any call for change in each national election over the past fifty years. It would be an understatement to see May 13 as an affair that has been sufficiently resolved by Malaysia with no social repercussions today. In fact, the negative impact of the tragedy has developed into a phenomenon of post-trauma that continues to haunt the psyche of the people of Malaysia, especially the Malays and the Chinese. Even in the last decade, namely, sixty years after Malaysia's Independent Day, Chinese Malaysians are still falling victim to socio-political isolation through statements such as "Chinese go back to China,"[1] "Chinese

---

are cheaters,"[2] "Boycott Chinese businesses,"[3] "Chinese are 'pendatang,'"[4] and so forth.

Studies on May 13 have not agreed as to the cause of the clashes. "The May 13 Tragedy" (1969) report produced by the National Operations Council denotes it as an "engineered tension" closely related to the seditious campaign speeches and victory processions by the opposition party[5] and also the preceding activities of the Labour Party of Malaya (LPM), which probably associated itself with the Communist Party of Malaya (MCP).[6] The report supports the perspective of the then Prime Minister Tunku Abdul Rahman Putra Al-Haj, who documented his accounts in his book entitled *13 Mei: Sebelum dan Selepas* (2007; revised in 2012). Former British officer Leon Comber perceived the tragic incident as an outbreak due to "historical circumstances," namely that the communal riots erupted when "Malay and Chinese emotions rubbed raw and came dangerously close to breaking point" (61). On the other hand, Dr Kua Kia Soong's *May 13: Declassified Documents on the Malaysian Riots of 1969* (2007), deriving its data from the declassified reports by the British Public Records Office, suggested that the riots were not to be understood as spontaneous acts of communal tensions or due to the subversive Communists but a purposeful bloodshed aimed at orchestrating a "coup d'état," namely that a segment of

---

2015 ("Baling MP Azeez Told to Retract "Balik Tongsan" Remark in Parliament," 2015). He later apologized and retracted his "balik Tongshan" remark. It was reiterated by Red Shirt Movement leader-cum-former Sungai Besar Umno Chief Dato' Sri Jamal Md Yunos ("Umno Man Claims Beijing Envoy's Comment Proves Chinese Malaysians Can Return to China," 2015).

2   "Your race are cheaters" is a quote from a press statement made by Red Shirt Movement Leader Mohd Ali Baharom on 22 December 2015 ("School Your Cheating Race, Ex-soldier Tells M'sia's Ruling Chinese Party," 2015).

3   A statement made by the then agriculture and agro-based industries minister Dato' Sri Ismail Sabri Yaacob in February 2015 ("Boycott Chinese Businesses to Lower Price of Goods, Minister Tells Malays," 2015).

4   "Pendatang" means "aliens" or "intruders" in the Malay language, and is a view held by radical Malays towards Chinese Malaysians.

5   "Victory Marches"; see Majlis 29-30.

6   "Engineered Tension"; see Majlis 27-28.

the radical Malays had aimed to discredit the moderate policies of Tunku Abdul Rahman (Kua 3).

While the "truth"s are being debated, this paper is more interested in examining the Malay and Chinese psyches with regard to the May 13 tragedy as reflected in their respective literature. In this study, a total of thirty-three literary works produced by Malay and Chinese writers since 1969 until the current year were examined and listed in Section II of the paper. Of this corpus of works, all nine literary works produced by Malay writers on the topic, without exception, ascribe to a prescriptive approach, while the twenty-three literary works produced by Chinese ethnic are mainly descriptive in nature with only two exceptions, namely Ding Yun's Chinese short story "A Village Under Siege" ("Wei Xiang," 1982) and Shirley Geok-lin Lim's English novel *Joss and Gold* (2001). "Prescriptive" refers to writings with a clear authorial intent to propagate racial harmony, national unity or a related cause. It's prescriptive because it's trying to suggest a "solution" or ideal pathway to track on, like doctors prescribing medication to their patients. On the other hand, "descriptive" relates to writings that dwell on the depiction of grief and agony of the main characters, reflecting some sort of defensiveness and fixation in the post-trauma stage. These different literary responses on the subject matter, namely the prescriptive versus the descriptive, point to the different attitudes and post-trauma responses of the respective ethnic community in their literature related to the May 13 tragedy.

Although a majority of these writers did not witness the incident themselves, the fear and pain that are tied to the event are relived in their works. In fact, even the "belated" grievances that the writers tried to express and what their readers would experience accordingly are as haunting as being placed at the scene. This perhaps, is why literary trauma theory associates trauma with the Freudian notion of "belatedness" (Mahan 94). As if dealing with "what happens upon waking up" (Caruth 64), writers attempt to unpack a traumatic event that was not fully understood or experienced at the time of occurrence in their writings. Among the proponents of the trauma theory, Michael Rothberg applied it to the analysis of the Jewish holocaust literature (Rothberg, 2000). Detailing Rothberg's analysis, William Mahan names anyone other than the surviving victims as the "bystanders" or the "latecomers." The bystanders feel "impelled to bear an impossible witness to the extreme from a place of relative safety" and the latecomers inherit the detritus of the traumatic times (Mahan 2). He argues that these groups of people will recount the incident from their post-memory and "post-trauma" or "post-post-trauma" position (1). Stemming from this notion of belated response and the aftermath of the May 13 trauma, this article will expound on the post-tragedy accounts of various Malay and Chinese writers through the decades until current days.

II.   Malay and Chinese Literature Written in Response to the May 13 Incident

THE nationwide state of Emergency immediately following May 13 was a significant drawback to the progress of Malaysia, which had just achieved her independence for a decade then. Also, there were strict guidelines and restrictions imposed by the authorities against discussions of May 13 in the public sphere. Nonetheless, the emotional impact of the incident still surfaces in quite a number of literary works produced by Malaysian writers between 1969 and 2019. In chronological order of publication, I managed to gather thirty-three literary works produced by Malay and Chinese writers in response to the May 13 tragedy. Of this pool of work, the written work by Abdullah Hussain, Ding Yun, Looi Yook Tho and Hanna Alkaf will be given a more in-depth analysis, as they reflect the respective Malay and Chinese ethnic mentalities in four respective eras that this article attempts to examine. Their perspectives on Malay-Chinese clashes relate to the generation they represent. Their propositions regarding racial relations in Malaysia dictate the differences in their writing approach, which will in turn influence their respective readers. First, let us run through my summary list of thirty-three works in response to May 13 that were produced by Malay and Chinese writers between 1969 and 2019:

A.   Between 1969 and 1979

1969 May: Usman Awang, "Kambing Hitam" [Scapegoat]. Poem.

Denouncement of the political manipulation that had killed the "scapegoats" in the name of racism, communism, extremism and gangsterism. (Prescriptive)

1969 May: Said Zahari, "Tangan-tangan yang tersembunyi" [Hidden Hands]. Poem.

Denouncement of the "hidden hands" that had shed the blood of the poor because of "colour, race, religion and language." (Prescriptive)

1969 July: Lai Jingwen, "Da Haojie" [Catastrophe]. Poem.

Lament on the utter desperation of a "city of death." (Descriptive)

1969 July: Lu Lang (Chen Zhengxin), "Shangkou" [The Wound]. Poem.

Lament on one's sufferings in a "thorny city," where the flora and even the rain have all turned "thorny." (Descriptive)

1969 July: Qian Qiu (Qiu Ruimao), "Xinxiang Licheng" [Emotional Journey]. Poem.

Lament on one's torturous entrapment under the debris of a fire. (Descriptive)

1969 Nov.: Gui Yan (Lin Benfa), "Mei Weiba de Shou" [The Beast without a Tail]. Poem.

Lament on the destruction caused by the ravaging selfishness of the "beast." (Descriptive)

1970 Feb.: Shahnon Ahmad, "Salam Sekeluarga" [Greetings to My Family]. Short Story.

Projection of undesirable outcome of the national election due to unreadiness of the majority voters. (Prescriptive)

1970 Mar.: Gui Yan (Lin Benfa),"Nakuai Furou" [That Piece of Rotten Meat]. Poem.

Lament on an infected skin ulcer as a euphemism for a black spot in history. (Descriptive)

1970 May: Shahnon Ahmad, "AI" (in Malay). Short Story.

Denouncement of the indifference of Malaysians abroad towards their home country. (Prescriptive)

1970 July: Zam Ismail, "Sebuah Jambatan" [A Bridge]. Poem.

Exhortation to embrace unity in diversity, using the analogy of a golden bridge. (Prescriptive)

1971: Abdullah Hussain, *Interlock*. Novel.

First published in Malay entitled *Interlok* in 1971. English translation was available in 2010; amended version published in 2012 after the novel was rejected by the Indian community due to its derogatory word use, i.e., "pariah" (outcast). **Projection** of how Malay, Chinese and Indian communities could possibly "interlock" into a cohesive Malayan society. (Prescriptive)

1973: A. Samad Said, "Benih Harapan" [Seed of Hope]. Poem.

Exhortation to embrace peace and equality, without which the independence of the country could not be fully appreciated. (Prescriptive)

1976: Ee Tiang Hong, "Kuala Lumpur, May 1969." Poem.

Depiction of a **bitter memory** of violence associated with the riot, imagery of solders in leopard-spot uniform, and the media being controlled by the authorities. (Descriptive)

1976: Ee Tiang Hong, "Requiem." Poem.

Expression of **deep grief** and **sorrow** even as time passes after the May 13 tragedy. (Descriptive)

B.   Between 1980 and 1989

1982: Ding Yun, "Wei Xiang" [A Village under Siege]. Short Story.

Portrayal of how people would voluntarily help each other in time of need **irrespective of skin colour**. Its Malay translation entitled "Terbelenggu di Kampung Halaman" was available in 1988. (Prescriptive)

1987: Poh Seng Titt, "Jinghum" [Shock]. Short Story.

Expression of **anguish** over the racial tensions in relation to the Private Adam shooting in 1987, juxtaposing it with the painful memory of May 13 in 1969. (Descriptive)

Note: The Malay writers were very much concerned about other issues during the 1980s, especially regarding charting new directions for Modern Malay Literature. No literary work related to May 13 tragedy was spotted.

C. Between 1990 and 1999

1990: Xiao Hei, *Qianxi [On the Eve]*. Novella.

Denouncement of the intensified conflicts among visionless Chinese leaders via a metaphor of the eruption of boils on a 513 victim who also contracted an eye disease due to the boils on her body. (Descriptive)

1992: Abdullah Hussain, "Melissa" (in Malay). Short Story.

Projection of how forgiveness and mutual acceptance could weather the test of racial extremism. (Prescriptive)

1994: Chuah Guat Eng, *Echoes of Silence*. Novel.

Depiction of a great sense of **displacement** in a Chinese that resulted in her choosing to migrate and leave Malaysia after the May 1969 incident. (Descriptive)

1999: Looi Yook Tho, "Duli Ri" [Independence Day]. Poem.

A **mockery** of the practice of "fair distribution" of the economic pie, which was built on an unjust basis, written from the perspective of protectionism of a certain ethnic group. (Descriptive)

D. From 2000

2000: Teo Hsu-Ming, *Love and Vertigo*. Novel.

The May 13 tragedy was depicted as the main **entanglement** that had caused her family to migrate. (Descriptive)

2000: Looi Yook Tho, "Zhishi Chuanle Yishuang Huang Wazi" [Just Because I'm Wearing a Pair of Yellow Socks]. Poem.

An **emotional outpouring** about one's less privileged position in one's country merely because of one's skin colour ("yellow socks"), tracked down to the history of inter-racial aggression on May 13. (Descriptive)

2001: Shirley Geok-lin Lim, *Joss and Gold*. Novel.

Casting of a vision of a new nation that is not tied to ethnicity. (Prescriptive)

2001: Ng Kim Chew, "Kai Wang Zhongguo de Man Chuan" [On a Slow Boat to China]. Short Story.

Depiction of **attackers**, **gun shots** and **special branch police** in the streets and, via an illusion of a character, a metaphoric imagery of a sailor boat filled with **dead bodies** of the Chinese sailing very slowly towards the Far East. (Descriptive)

2006: Looi Yook Tho, "Wo de Wuyisan" [My Account of 513]. Poem.

Depiction of decades-old **emotional suppression**, being "silenced" from mentioning 513, and the unjust sociopolitical "crossbars" imposed on the non-Malays. (Descriptive)

2007: Ding Yun, *Chidao Jung Zhe* [*The Horror of the Equator*]. Novel.

Vivid description of the **violent attacks** between Malays and Chinese during the May 13 outbreak. (Descriptive)

2009: Lin Jianwen, "Zai Yuhai Shang Kegu" [Carving on the Fishbones]. Poem.

An **overly** calm depiction of the loss of lives on May 13, the double standard imposed on the citizens wearing "yellow socks" (quoting Looi), and a documentation of such experiences on oracle or fish bones. (Descriptive)

2010: Li Tianbao, *Qiluo Xiang* [*Romance of Malaya*]. Novel.

Expression of an attitude when relating the May 13 tragedy: Depiction of a maidservant shutting the doors and windows of the house when sensing that major **turmoil** was happening on the streets. (Descriptive)

2012: Li Zishu, *Gaobie de Niandai* [*An Era of Farewell*]. Novel.

The story starts from page 513, depicting a lady whose life was altered after she encountered a life-threatening incident on May 13. There is no 'secret' to be discovered in this story, if the readers expect any. As if there was a total loss of memory, the 'missing pages' are indications of **deliberate denial** of trauma. (Descriptive)

2014: Ho Sok Fong, "Si Ren Zhaoguo" [Marsh of Dead] in *Migong Tanzi* [Maze Carpet]. Short Story.

Haunting description of the **crushed skull, deformed human face** and **ruptured intestines** of a female subject that refused to breathe her last despite being murdered over and over again. (Descriptive)

2015: Hafizah Iszahanid, *Bukan Orangorang* [*We're Not Scarecrows*]. Novel.

The onset of the story was about Malay-Chinese racial conflicts in 1969, relating to the divisive ideologies and political campaigns during the era; **exhortation** for all to be "humans, not scarecrows." (Prescriptive)

2018: Looi Yook Tho, "1969 Nian Wuyue" [May 1969]. Poem.

Lament of the loss of lives during May 13, and expression of **cynicism** about those with vested interests, presented in pictorial form. (Descriptive)

2019: Hanna Alkaf, *The Weight of Our Sky*. Novel.

Projection of how one's courage to extend kindness to people of different backgrounds and doing "what is right" is desired for the nation to withstand the weight of racial conflicts. (Prescriptive)

* Four authors from the abovementioned, namely Abdullah Hussain, Ding Yun, Looi Yook Tho, Hanna Alkaf, and their respective works are discussed at length in Sections III, IV, V, and VI of this article.

Between 1969 and 1979: This list contains works produced during the first decade following the May 13 incident, i.e., the decade when memories were still fresh and pains were still felt. Chinese poems such as "Holocaust," "The Wound" and "Emotional Journey" were all descriptive in nature, describing the grief or horror of the incident. Surprisingly, Malay poems entitled "Scapegoat," "Hidden Hands," and "Seed of Hope," along with short stories such as "Greetings to My Family" and "Al," as well as the novel Interlok were all written in a prescriptive manner, namely with a clear authorial intent to promote unity of the nation, with an emphasis on the common good of all people over ethnic differences. For this era, Abdullah Hussain's novel *Interlok* (1971; English translation, *Interlock* 2010) will be discussed at length in Section III of the paper.

Between 1980 and 1989: This is the decade following the introduction of the New Economic Policy (NEP).[7] Malay writers sought out to incorporate new themes and styles in their writings and worked diligently towards regional recognition. Almost none revisited the topic of May 13. However, that was not the case with Chinese writers, who continued to wrestle on the subject matter until today. During this era, Ding Yun, for example, produced his award-winning and well-received short story entitled "A Village Under Siege" ("Wei Xiang," 1982). Its unusual prescriptive approach found favour with Dewan Bahasa dan Pustaka (DBP),[8] and was thus translated into the Malay language by DBP in 1988 with the title "Terbelenggu di Kampung Halaman." This work will be discussed at length in Section IV of the paper.

Between 1990 and 1999: During this era of Prime Minister Dr. Mahathir Mohamad,[9] the booming economic growth of the country did not wipe out the post-memory of May 13. The subject matter surfaced in the poems produced by Looi Yook Tho, who is often referred to as the prince of Chinese Malaysian poetry writing. Abdullah Hussain wrote specifically on the topic. The literary works of the former were predominantly descriptive in nature, while those of the latter were highly prescriptive. Abdullah Hussain and Looi will be discussed at length in Section III and Section V respectively.

From 2000: In the new millennium, Malaysian writers of all languages still published on the topic. Their post-trauma accounts on the bloodshed incident have gained international attention. In

---

7   The New Economic Policy (NEP) is a social-reengineering programme implemented by the Malaysian government during 1971 to 1990 in order to eradicate poverty and eliminate the identification of race with economic functions. It has always been criticized for its overt favoritism of the Malays to the effect of relegating the non-Malays in the country to second-class citizens.

8   DBP is a statutory body whose functions include the development of language and literature, especially on promotion of the Malay language.

9   Tun Dr. Mahathir Mohamad is the 4th and 7th (2018-2020) Prime Minister of Malaysia. He was successful in creating economic success for Malaysia his first term as Prime Minister (1981-2003), especially during the 1990s, which he boosted Malaysian national pride with a new academic term, namely, "The Malaysian Race (Bangsa Malaysia)."

fact, the latest novel on May 13 is Hanna Alkaf's *The Weight of Our Sky*, published by Simon & Schuster in 2019. Hanna Alkaf will be discussed at length in Section VI of the paper.

III.   Abdullah Hussain's *Interlok* (1971) and "Melissa" (1992)

MALAYSIAN National Laureate Abdullah Hussain (1920–2014) devoted close attention to the issue of interracial relations in his novel *Interlok* (1971; its English translation entitled *Interlock* was published in 2010) and, concerning the May 13 tragedy, in his short story "Melissa" (1992). Two things are notable about Abdullah Hussain. First, he was enlisted in a three-month training at the Syonan Koa Kunrenzo (Japanese Training Institute for Senior Officers) during the Japanese Occupation, resulting in his pro-Japan orientation. In his own words, his "fanatical" nationalist idealism had caused him to believe that in helping the Japanese, the European colonial powers could be overthrown, as how the Dutch fell to the Japanese in Sumatra and Jawa.[10] Second, Abdullah Hussain adhered to the "art for society" motto, which was propagated by the Malay writers' movement known as "Angkatan Sasterawan 50," or ASAS '50, during the era. Besides believing that official use of the Malay language would promote the unity of Malaysia as a nation, Abdullah Hussain, like his other Muslim Malay colleagues, also saw Malay literature as a means to influence readers towards goodness and Allah SWT.[11]

Abdullah Hussain's award-winning historical fiction entitled *Interlok* was published not long after the May 13 incident. *Interlok* does not depict the May 13 incident per se but offers an honest examination of the historical divisive factors that had kept the

10   See Abdullah Hussain (2000: 307). The text was a project paper presented at the National Writers General Dialogue session, known as "Dialog Agung Bersama Sasterawan Negara," at the DBP Seminar Room on 26 February 2000. The session was organized by the Kuala Lumpur Writers Association, known as Persatuan Penulis Kuala Lumpur or KALAM and Dewan Bahasa & Pustaka.

11   See Abdullah Hussain (2000: 288). The text was the transcript of Abdullah Hussain's acceptance speech for his National Literary Award at Anugerah Sastera Negara ke-8 in 1996.

Indians, Malays and Chinese in Malaysia apart. The novel depicts how the British's "divide and rule" policy succeeded in creating hardliners among the Malays, owing to their less-favoured economic status. In the story, when the Japanese invade Peninsular Malaya, Lazim, one of the Malay leaders, tells the villagers, "We must help the Japanese. If the British pass our village, we must arrest them and turn them over to the Japanese." He says, "They (referring to the Japanese) are the ones who have chased away the white people. And one day, we will rule our own country" (Abdullah Hussain 2012: 318-319).

As reflected in *Interlok*, the Malays had also projected their hatred of the colonial government onto the local Chinese, perceiving them as people of pagan religions who gathered wealth from the Malays via shrewd tricks. At that time, there were cases of Malays losing their mortgaged properties to the white capitalists due to their inability to pay off their accumulated debts. It was a time when the banking and legal systems were not fully understood. In *Interlok*, we learn that Seman's father has mortgaged his house to Cina Panjang, the tall Chinese "*taukeh* (small business owner)." Even though Cina Panjang can produce evidence of the signed documents, what transpired between the two parties is not entirely convincing, since Seman has never seen it and heard anything related to it from his dad: "Seman began to think about Cina Panjang. Wouldn't it be good if the Japanese arrested him? Then the paddy lands could be returned to the [original] owners" (Abdullah Hussain 2012: 318).

Eventually, at the end of *Interlok* all three ethnic groups, namely the Malays, Indians and Chinese, learn to accept each other and begin to understand their new roles in the newly formed country named Malaya while ushering in Malayan Independence Day on 31 August 1957. Here, Abdullah Hussain projected a strong desire of all the peoples "to form a single Malayan society, where everybody could live in peace and harmony" (2012: 406). Yew Seng, the second son of Cina Panjang, was portrayed as a prototype of a younger generation of Chinese Malaysians whose love for Malaysia and friendliness towards the Malays were genuine.

Abdullah Hussain's short story "Melissa" was a work that reflected upon the May 13 tragedy. It is about a Chinese female university student, Melissa, who chooses the May 13 riots as her undergraduate research project. In the story, Abdullah Hussain created two model characters: an unnamed Chinese woman who extends forgiveness to the Malay people who murdered her fiancé during the May 13 outbreak, and Melissa, the protagonist, who also loses her Muslim boyfriend that day. Abdullah Hussain appraised the former as follows:

> [...] Such is a true Malaysian woman, a result of this blessed land, for she has not the slightest regret. To her Malay colleague who caused her to lose her fiancé she bears no grudge but continues to remain close-knit like real relatives. She also does not regret the scar on her face that, because it was beyond her will, forced to become a spinster. (1997: 670)[12]

As for Melissa, Abdullah Hussain gave her an interrogative role. Melissa questions, "Why were there riots? Why should people living in a peaceful country suddenly strike and kill each other? Why must the Chinese kill the Malays and Malays kill the Chinese? Why?" (2012: 668).

In "Melissa," Abdullah Hussain concluded that the seed of interracial rivalry was but the "virus implanted by the colonial government," which is the "racial polarization virus" (2012: 672). Subsequently, Abdullah Hussain validated the local identity of the Chinese in Malaysia. He wrote, "[Melissa] cannot live in China, even though she speaks Chinese, adheres to Chinese culture and her ancestors were immigrants from Guangdong [...] Their mentalities are different" (2012: 680). Thus, back in 1992, Abdullah Hussain had already offered a counterargument to those who instigated the Chinese Malaysians to "return to China (*balik ke Negeri China*)." To

---

12   The following quotes are my translations from the original texts in the Malay language.

date, Malaysia has been the cherished birthplace and home country for at least four generations of Chinese. All in all, Abdullah Hussain's writing somehow became the benchmark for Malay writers in adopting the prescriptive approach in resolving interracial conflicts in their literature.

IV. Ding Yun's "A Village Under Siege" (1982) and *The Horror of the Equator* (2007)

DING Yun is the pen name of Chen Chun An. He was one of the first Chinese Malaysian writers who dealt with the May 13 issue in novels and short stories. Contrary to the common misconception that Chinese Malaysians are all well-to-do city folk, Ding Yun was born to an impecunious family in Klang, Selangor. As he could not pay his school fees of RM7.50, he had to quit schooling after completing his primary education. He worked at a wood factory in Hulu Langat. Ding Yun was first recognized for his "estate stories," which had the themes of death, stupidity, ill-treatment by oppressors and so forth. Born in the 1950s, Ding Yun and his contemporaries remembered two major incidents that pricked the ethnic sensitivities of the different races after Malaysia's Independence, namely, May 13 and "Operation Lalang."[13] Ding Yun himself suffered physical and emotional separation from his mother and eight siblings during the May 13 incident.

Engaging May 13 as its theme, Ding Yun's "A Village Under Siege" earned him the first prize in the short story category of the Literature Competition jointly organized by the Chinese Malaysian Writers Association and the *Malayan Thung Pau Daily News* in 1982. It tells the story of Lin Tuo, who lives with his father and

---

13 "Operation Lalang" was the second largest crackdown by the Royal Police Malaysia since the May 13 disturbance. Political suspects such as NGO activists, opposition politicians and intellectuals were detained without trial under the Internal Security Act (ISA). It also involved the revoking of publication licences of two newspapers, *The Star* and *Sin Chew Jit Poh*, as well as two weeklies, *The Sunday Star* and *Watan*.

sister in a suburban village with Malays and native tribes as their neighbours. The unpretentious thought processes of Lin Tuo are a good representation of the simple minds of a majority of suburban dwellers who do not see the impending danger to their lives immediately following the 3rd Malaysian General Election:

> [...] He doubts what chaotic situation could have taken place in such poor and remote areas like theirs. The Malays, Chinese, or the native people have all tagged along well to earn their living together all this while. Working together, they have small conflicts from time to time. But violence? Killing of each other? That could only happen among sophisticated city people, right? (Ding, 1982)[14]

During the outbreak of May 13 in the city, many Chinese families who lived adjacent to the Malays evacuated their villages to avoid any looming sectarian clashes. However, there is an interesting twist to the story of the escape of Lin Tuo's family. Halfway through, they decide to turn back to their home because Lin's father, a man who had always toiled on the soil, insists that he cannot leave his ploughs behind. Lo and behold, there is another twist to the story at the end: Torches show up at their gate, and when it seems altogether impossible for the Lins to run away this time, the "intruders" in the dark present themselves—they are Lin's Malay neighbours Samad and Mohammad, who have run out of food supplies. Equally afraid of being slain by any armed mob, the two men came over hoping to get a share of any edibles such as tapioca or beans. Ding Yun's writing approach in "A Village Under Siege" was prescriptive in nature. His authorial intent was clear: To safeguard the well-being of everybody, regardless of skin colour and social background, sectarian activities should be curbed while mutual acceptance of each other should be promoted.

---

14   My English translation from the original Chinese text.

Ding Yun's novel, *The Horror of the Equator* (*Chidao jingzhe*), on the other hand, is highly descriptive in nature, which was a common writing approach of Chinese writers in historical accounts. In this novel, Ding Yun described May 13 as a memory of "reds", namely red wired gate, red soil, red well water, heads detached from bodies, and, patches of blood stains of the murdered. He also documented that the May 13 violence began in Kuala Lumpur and impacted Melaka, Penang and other cities swiftly. He reported that the Malay-Chinese clashes had caused houses, shops, schools and cars to be set on fire: "About 300 people lost their lives during the bloodshed that lasted from the 13th to the 18th. Some were killed by gunshots from armed soldiers. The number of arrests easily came up to more than 3,000" (Ding 2007: 73-75). In short, Ding Yun engaged the descriptive approach to recount the grievances related to the Malay-Chinese clashes on May 13, 1969.

V.   Looi Yook Tho's "My Account of 513" (2006), "May, 1969" (2023) and Related Poems

AS a matter of fact, Chinese Malaysian writers have never shed off their May 13 anxiety in their writings. Even today, poet Looi Yook Tho still writes extensively on the topic. Born in Penang and a software engineer by profession, Looi has won many Chinese literature awards for his poems.[15] Notable for his linguistic recreation and avant-garde writing style, Looi has also written political poems that depict the difficulties Chinese Malaysians experienced under the social-reengineering program implemented by the Malaysian government since the 1970s. The repeated symbolism he employed in this respect included "the yellow socks" and "the

---

15   Looi's literary awards include the Taiwan Times Literature Award, Malaysia Huazong ("Floral Trail") Literature Award, Malaysia Outstanding Young Writers Award, and Malaysia Hai-O ("Seagull") Writers Award. His poetry collections include *Zai Wo Wanneng de Xiangxiang Guodu (In My Wonderful Imaginary Kingdom*, 1999), *Huang Wazi Zibian Shu (An Apology for the Yellow Socks*, 2008), and *Xunjia (Search for a Home*, 2013).

high jump crossbars."[16] At least four of Looi's poems depicted the May 13 tragedy graphically. His picture poem entitled "May, 1969" (2023), for example, gives an account via three calendars of three respective groups in relation to the tragedy, namely the "winning" side (i.e., the ones who have successfully erased May 13 from the calendar of the year); the families of the May 13 victims (i.e., parents whose memory of the month consists of nothing but May 13); and the political opportunists who use May 13 as their rhetoric to manipulate the people (i.e., every day thenceforth becomes May 13). Kindly refer to page 68 for the poem.

Another poem by Looi entitled "My Account of May 13," which contains 58 lines altogether, provided more poetic imageries of the incident. An abstract of the poem is as follows:

I don't remember seeing any blood that day
In my mother's womb, my dream
Was shattered
By a heart hammering louder than fleeing footsteps
My memory fails me
Was it a war drum, or was it my own heartbeat?

The icy corpses of the dead
And the questioning lips of the living
One by one, all are buried under the sanctions of the Statute

Silenced childhood, silenced roads
Silenced army camps, silenced *kopitiams*
Silenced telephone booths, silenced libraries
Silenced badminton courts, silenced journals
Silenced asylums
Silenced mother[17]

16　The "yellow socks" symbolism has also found influence in poet Lin Jianwen's anthology, *Mao Zhu Zai Yizuo Redai Yuanshi Senlin (A Cat That Lives in a Tropical Jungle*, 2009).

17　This poem was first published in the 2nd June 2006 issue of the magazine *Jiaofeng*. It was then selected and included in Looi Yook Tho, *Xunjia* [*Searching for a Home*], and also in Tian, Wang & Looi: 238-240.

"May, 1969"

History Book of the "Winning"

MON	TUE	WED	THU	FRI	SAT	SUN
			1	2	3	4
5	6	7	8	9	10	11
12		14	15	16	17	18
19	20	21	22	23	24	25
26	27	28	29	30	31	

Calendar of the Mothers after the Onslaught on Their Children
Following the Mother's Day Celebration

MON	TUE	WED	THU	FRI	SAT	SUN
				□	□	□
□	□	□	□	□	□	□
□	13	□	□	□	□	□
□	□	□	□	□	□	□
□	□	□	□	□	□	

Ever-repeated Gimmicks of Those with Vested Interests

MON	TUE	WED	THU	FRI	SAT	SUN
			1	2	3	4
5	6	7	8	9	10	11
12	13	13	13	13	13	13
13	13	13	13	13	13	13
13	13	13	13	13	13	

(Looi 2023: 99-100)

Towards the end of the poem, Looi complained that: "This city has borne too much historical baggage / Burdened by too many matters of the heart / Unable to put them down / Let's have a 513 memorial garden, shall we?" The excruciating pain of May 13 also found its way in two other poems by Looi. In "Independence Day" (1999), he wrote, "On a rainy day that followed / Truth contested with spears and parang knives / The blood of our father and the Chinese people / Treaded along the edge of the same knife / The red of the hibiscus. The blood on the roads" (Tian, Wang & Looi 238-240).

In "Just because I'm Wearing a Pair of Yellow Socks," Looi portrayed himself as a terrified fetus hidden in his mother's womb:

> I lie hidden in the amniotic fluid of my mother's womb
> Her heartbeats quicken as the Malay kompang drums roar
> In a rubber estate of deafening silence, she takes shelter
> From the parang knives of the lying officers
> [...]
> The shedding of the same blood always repeats on May 13
> On the peninsular on the Equator where Truth was twisted
> The violent mob with erect penises kicked aside the Law
> And ejaculated the sperm of anarchism
> Into the womb of a maiden forbidden to use her mother
> tongue freely
> Just because, her mother was wearing a pair of yellow socks?
> A chill wind from the forest of multiculturalism
> Throws me back to that year, that day
> [...]
> when this land flowed with blood (Looi 2008: 42-52)

All in all, the intense traumatic expressions relating to the violence of the crime scene have been a fixation in Looi's memory, which altogether represented the wounded psyche of many Chinese Malaysians, even today.

VI.   Hanna Alkaf's *The Weight of Our Sky*

A recipient of the D.K. Dutt Award for Literary Excellence, Hanna Alkaf gained attention among literary critics with her youth fiction *The Weight of Our Sky* (2019), which deals with the May 13 tragedy. She is probably the first Malay writer who chose to write in English on the topic. Her novel tells of a Eurasian teenage girl named Melati Ahmad who is traumatized by a djinn that keeps threatening her with the sight of her mother being murdered mercilessly. This djinn plays the role of the devil's advocate to distort Melati's sensibility. It also serves as a literary device to facilitate Hanna's language of magical realism. When grotesque images of people being killed constantly appear in Melati's hallucinations, the cruelty of sectarian mobs and the destruction during the May 13 tragedy can thus be presented liberally.

As the novel was written for youths, Hanna employed the prescriptive approach: She presented two near-flawless model characters, namely Melati's mom and Auntie Bee. Melati never knew Auntie Bee beforehand, but it is under the roof of Auntie Bee that Melati, together with other survivors, finds refuge on that ill-fated day. On the other hand, Melati's mom has to move around with her medical team to attend to patients even as she has no clue of her own daughter's whereabouts. Here, the sacrificial services of both of these ladies are portrayed as the outworking of their faith in God. In the novel, Melati's mom is known for her fervent prayers, symbolized by her beautiful prayer mat. As for Auntie Bee, her devotedness to Jesus Christ is symbolized by the wooden cross on her wall. Hanna's prescriptive approach in showcasing the respect for the faith and religious practices of others was quite commendable. Another thought-provoking pointer in *The Weight of Our Sky* is the question of who was to be blamed for the casualties in the tragedy. The protagonist has a constant struggle with self-blame: "She's (Melati's mom) going to die, and it's your (Melati's) fault" (Hanna 261). This nagging blame game will eventually lead readers to reckon that there is no definite answer to the "whose fault" question but that it is a collective historical burden for every Malaysian.

VII. Conclusion

AFTER a tragic incident, a person will naturally encounter experiences such as denial, anger, constant bargaining of if-onlys, grief and depression. Many may eventually recover if they are able to nurse their feelings and reframe their perspective of the tragedy they suffered personally. However, not everyone can manage to relate to those who have failed their trust. Forgiveness is one aspect; recovery of the inner being is another. In the post-trauma stage, one's denial of the tragedy and isolation from others, for example, may turn into acute pain and long-lasting bitterness. The descriptive language of pain and the defensive tones in Chinese Malaysian writings on the topic of May 13, to a certain extent, reflect their emotional and psychological fixation on the post-trauma stage. This 'wounded' language somewhat became the ingrained DNA of Chinese Malaysian writings. On the other hand, modern-day Malay writers, though continually adhering to the prescriptive formula of promoting humanity above other authorial intents from "Day One," are not too naïve to neglect the post-traumatic repercussions of May 13. Five decades after the tragedy and even today, it is still a nagging racial harmony issue that Malay writers will not give up hope on engaging.

Of the corpus of literature related to May 13, Abdullah Hussain and Ding Yun represent two different generations born before Malaysia's Independence Day. Looi Yook Tho and Hanna Alkaf represent Generation X and Generation Y (a.k.a. the Millennials), respectively, namely two generations born after Independence. As discussed in Section III, Abdullah Hussain represented the generation that adhered to the "art for society" slogan of the ASAS '50 writers' guild, which subsequently laid the ground for the Malay language and religion of Islam to shape the core identity of Malaysia. His prescriptive approach makes provisions for other ethnic groups to participate in the nation-building process of Malay(si)a, but under those delineated terms. Ding Yun represents the generation born during the decade when Malaysia attained Independence from the British and began her engine of self-governance. This generation witnessed the May 13 tragedy, and was subdued by the State of Emergency as well as tight control over potentially "subversive elements" in published works. As discussed in Section IV, Ding Yun's "A Village Under Siege" (1982) is probably one of the very few pieces of Chinese literature on the topic that employed the prescriptive approach, envisioning open communal interactions between different ethnic groups. Poet Looi Yook Tho represents the generation that first underwent the NEP launched by Tun Abdul Razak. The ethnic Chinese experienced hardship due to stringent quotas under the NEP limiting their enrolment in public universities as well as job placements in the civil service. Since then, the ethnic Chinese could not help but suffer an inferiority complex and see themselves as "second-class citizens" in their own country of birth. This whining mentality was described vividly in all four of Looi's poems discussed in Section V. Last but not least, as discussed in Section VI, Hanna Alkaf represents the modern educated Malays who want to chart new pathways for dialogue, especially on the issue of ethnic differences and disharmony. Her prescriptive approach in literature, namely to engage principles of humanity when tackling teething issues of racial conflict, is nevertheless benchmarked against those guidelines set by the founding generations of Malay writers.

Looking ahead, so long as Chinese Malaysians still experience unequal opportunities during the application for government jobs or studying at public universities, the descriptive grievances over the May 13 tragedy as exemplified in Looi's poems will still find an outlet in the contemporary Chinese literary sphere. On the other hand, the prescriptive approach adhered by Malay writers from "Day One" will probably not change, as the confidence of the Malays as the majority ethnic group in the country, with their special privileges as "Bumiputera" or the indigenous people of the land, is firmly secured and protected under the federal constitution. The difference in the political status of the Malay and Chinese languages, and the perspectives of the Malays and the Chinese regarding the bloodshed on May 13, 1969, has altogether resulted in differing approaches in their respective literary works in the post-May 13 era, even today. The difference between the Malays and Chinese in recounting the tragedy reflects the differing extent of their post-trauma stages. With the ill-memory of May 13 still deep within the psyche of both the Malay and Chinese ethnic groups in Malaysia, it will not be a surprise if the May 13 theme recurs in the newly published books written by young Malaysians.

WORKS CITED

Abdullah Hussain (1997) *Dari Kota Cahaya* (Kuala Lumpur: Dewan Bahasa & Pustaka).

Abdullah Hussain (2000) *Pertemuan Abadi: Koleksi Terpilih Abdullah Hussain* (Kuala Lumpur: Dewan Bahasa & Pustaka).

Abdullah Hussain (2012) *Interlock* [1971]. Trans. Hazizi Hamzah & Hashim Yaacob (Kuala Lumpur: Dewan Bahasa & Pustaka).

"Baling MP Azeez Told to Retract "Balik Tongsan" Remark in Parliament" (2015). *The Star*, 4 Nov. (www.thestar.com.my/news/nation/2015/11/04/abdul-azees-baling-retract-remark-pandikar).

"Boycott Chinese Businesses to Lower Price of Goods, Minister Tells Malays" (2015). *Malay Mail*, 2 Feb. (www.malaymail.com/news/malaysia/%202015/02/02/boycott-chinese-businesses-to-lower-price-of-goods-minister-tells-malays/832557).

Caruth, Cathy (1996) *Unclaimed Experience: Trauma, Narrative, and History* (Baltimore: Johns Hopkins University Press).

Comber, Leon (2012) *May 13 1969: The Darkest Day in Malaysian History* (Selangor: Marshall Cavendish Edition).

Ding Yun (1982) "Wei Xiang" [A Village Under Siege], Part I. 28 Dec. (www.sgwritings.com/14992/viewspace_45025.html).

Ding Yun (2007) *Chidao Jingzhe* [*The Horror of the Equator*] (Kuala Lumpur: Semarak Publishing Co.).

Hanna Alkaf (2019) *The Weight of Our Sky* (New York: Salaam Read).

Kua Kia Soong (2007) *May 13: Declassified Documents on the Ma-*

laysian Riots of 1969 (Kuala Lumpur: SUARAM).

Looi Yook Tho (2008) *Huang Wazi Zibian Shu* [*An Apology for the Yellow Socks*] (Kuala Lumpur: Got One Publisher).

Looi Yook Tho (2023) *Yi Ge Ren de Dushi* [*City of A Loner*] (Kuala Lumpur: Got One Publisher).

Mahan, William (2017) "Triangulating Trauma: Constellations of Memory, Representation, and Distortion in Elie Wiesel, Wolfgang Borchert, and W.G. Sebald." *Humanities* 6.4 (Nov.): 94-104.

Majlis Gerakan Negara (1969) *The May 13 Tragedy* (Kuala Lumpur: Jabatan Chetak Negara).

Rothberg, Michael (2000) *Traumatic Realism: The Demands of Holocaust Representation* (Minneapolis: University of Minnesota Press).

"School Your Cheating Race, Ex-soldier Tells M'sia's Ruling Chinese Party" (2015). *TODAY*, 22 Dec. (www.todayonline.com/world/asia/school-your-cheating-race-ex-soldier-tells-msias-ruling-chinese-party).

Tian Si, Wang Tao & Looi Yook Tho (2015) *Shoujie Fang Xiu Wenxue-Jiang Huojiang Zuopinji: Shige Juan* [*The First Fang Xiu Prize in Literature: A Collection of Prize Winning Poems*] (Singapore: Global Publishing Co.).

"Umno Man Claims Beijing Envoy's Comment Proves Chinese Malaysians Can Return to China" (2015). *Malay Mail*, 29 Sept. (www.malaymail.com/news/malaysia/2015/09/29/umno-man-claims-beijing-envoys-comment-proves-chinese-malaysians-can-return/978655).).

"Do Cultures Leak into Each Other?"
Polycultural Considerations in Selected Malaysian Anglophone and Sinophone Texts

SIM Wai Chew

> The sea was deep green, the colour of old, dark jade. That was the first time I ever noticed my skin, the colour of it. Not brown, not yellow, not white, not anything against the rich and mysterious green of the water around me.
>
> ——Tash Aw, *The Harmony Silk Factory* (2005)

IN a recent article addressing Malaysian Literature in English (MLE), Kavitha Ganesan argues cogently that scholars working in this domain may take heart from thematic overlaps between three life-writing works published between 2002 and 2007.[1] Written by three women authors of, respectively, Malay, Chinese, and Indian descent, the works appear to reproduce the social fissures that characterise the formation. The first text deploys a "nationalist" stance that potentially strengthens social exclusion while the latter two rehearse minority-diasporic allegiances that resist such exclusion, in particular the avowal that Malaysia's settler populations don't actually belong because they are, to use the local term, "*pendatang*" (new arrivals), or else the avowal that their belonging is merely juridical compared to the autochthonous population who are the true "sons [and] daughters of the soil" (Ganesan 170, 173). Nevertheless, Ganesan argues, the fact that these dyadic positions are constructed through

---

1 The three texts discussed by Ganesan are: Adibah Amin's *This End of the Rainbow* (2006), Christine Wu Ramsay's *Days Gone By: Growing Up in Penang* (2007), and Muthammal Palanisamy's *From Shore to Shore* (2002).

the use of nature imagery—through depictions of the sea, rivers, tropical flora, rainstorms, plantation monoculture and the like—suggests that "nature is as central as nationalist and diasporic agencies" in the self-delineation undertaken in these works (174). Such attributes amount to "a trend towards commonality" and bespeak "fundamental similarities" between the different groups (171,179). As "emergent moments" they may provide solutions to "new... more challenging issues" confronting MLE in the future, thus "allowing it to overcome the confines of ethnicity"; and overall this suggests that the field's trajectory "lies towards a promising future," Ganesan asserts in the conclusion to her essay, "not just within the local literary landscape but also within the larger framework of postcolonial studies" (179-80).

In this essay, I would like to sketch a theoretical propaedeutic to the putative trajectory identified by Ganesan, while also extending her claim to include Malaysian Literature in Chinese (MLC). Ganesan's claim that writerly engagements with nature—here taken as a metonym for "Green" thought in general—constitute emergent rationalities "crucial for the continuous growth and expansion of MLE" sounds plausible and appealing (180). But how such a move is to be accomplished is left largely unanswered. In the context of eco-crisis, nature engagement and relationality include the public virtues of stewardship and conservation. Its obverse, environmental degradation, may act as a rallying point for different constituencies to come together. Existential, health, and quality-of-life concerns raised by such despoliation may foster the creation of a common culture that moves beyond the "confines" of ethnic particularity, and this I argue is precisely the consideration proffered by a text published around the same time as the mentioned life-writing works, namely K.S. Maniam's Anglophone novel *Between Lives*. Detailing the travails of a government official tasked with reversing a deemed "obstructive" use of land by an elderly lady, this text encourages a consideration of what constitutes genuine "development" and what needs to be conserved. Another text which delves into these issues is Chuah Guat Eng's Anglophone novel *Days of Change*. Published in 2010, *Days of Change* delineates the existential challenges faced by a real-estate developer who reassesses his life after he falls down a ravine and hurts his head. It shows him fashioning an alternative notion of "development," one that questions our over-reliance on hegemonic formulations of the last.

Through a reading of *Between Lives, Days of Change*, and two MLC short stories written by, respectively, Li Zishu and Hai Fan, I argue that an important feature of recent MLE and MLC texts is their focus on cross-cultural synthesis as both a key social imperative and an arena providing some needed answers to the existential challenges posed by eco-crisis. Timothy Luke has suggested that "environmental justice movement[s], site defense organizations... and NIMBY ('not in my backyard') coalitions at the local level" can all be seen as "vital expressions" of popular political impulses (7). I use the term (eco-) popular as opposed to "populist" to designate the trend towards commonality spotted by Ganesan, and as rehearsed in the works discussed below. Abjuring hermetic or monadic notions of self and other, these works prompt our consideration by situating intergroup relations within a larger existential imperative to re-build human engagement and relationality with nature. For the mentioned syncretisms to thrive (or to even be noticed), however, I believe that we must adopt in an amended manner historian Vijay Prashad's notion of polyculturalism, which affirms that our cultural "lineages" are multiple rather than singular. For Prashad, polyculturalism names a situation in which a kind of "horizontal assimilation" between cultural entities is possible because it is based on the assumption that "people live coherent lives that are made up of a host of lineages" (xii). His insights are important because he proffers a dynamic notion of identity, and so avers that an unprepossessing status quo is capable of changing. The critical and pedagogical payback of engaging with this work is that it can counter the sway of neo-traditional currents in intellectual and social life, insofar as they tend to inhibit cross-cultural exchange by purveying hermetic notions of identity. Under its purview, as I attempt to show below, it can delineate an inclusive imaginary that helps to improve intergroup relations. Dwelling a moment with how Prashad substantiates his argument is thus important because it allows us to appreciate the significance of the border-crossing acts enacted in recent MLE and MLC works.

Dynamic Identities

IN his important 2001 book, *Everybody Was Kung Fu Fighting: Afro-Asian Connections and the Myth of Cultural Purity*, Prashad argues that the current dominant framework for conceiving and managing diversity, namely liberal multiculturalism, preserves at the level of "culture" conceived as a *sui generis* lineage the biological determinism that fuels coloniality, hegemonic racism (white supremacy), and, indeed, many non-white or subaltern varieties of racism. Multiculturalism, for Prashad, "refuses to accept that biology is destiny, but... smuggles in culture to do much the same thing" (xi). Its diktat means that we tend towards "a static view of history, with cultures already forged and with people enjoined to respect and tolerate each cultural world" (66). But this then generates familiar, vexed questions which plague both the academy and "our everyday interactions," questions such as: "Who defines the boundaries of culture or allows for change? Do cultures leak into each other? Can a person from one culture critique another culture?" (xi). Reservations about multiculturalism have also been tabled by other theorists such as Meer and Modood. For them the separatist construals of culture authorized by multiculturalism is problematic because a stress on "coexistence" comes arguably at the expense of "interaction and dialogue"; such a stance is too "groupist" in orientation, too "[c]ulture-[b]ound" or unyielding of synthesis; and furthermore it lacks "a sense of whole, in terms of such things as societal cohesion and national citizenship" (177, 185).

Prashad shares this view, and argues that postcolonial historians should therefore accentuate "cultural complexity" (66). His or her work is not to "carve out [different] lineages but to make sense of how people live culturally dynamic lives" replete with complex histories of engagement, intermixture and conflict (xii). Intellectual work in this arena should help us to recognise that "the cultures we produce are multifaceted and multivalent, that they borrow from as much as they tend to disagree with each other" (36). Prashad bids us to consider in this regard:

> the rebel Africans, who fled the slave plantations in the Americas and took refuge among the Amerindians to create communities such as the Seminoles'; the South Asian workers who jumped ship in eighteenth-century Salem, Massachusetts, to enter the black community; Frederick Douglass's defense of Chinese "coolie" laborers in the nineteenth century; the interactions of the Black Panther Party with the Red Guard and the Brown Berets in the mid-twentieth century; and finally the multiethnic working-class gathering in the new century. (x)

Pertinent to the issue of fostering pluralism in the Nusantara world,[2] Prashad also bids us to revivify the solidarities forged during the 1955 Afro-Asian conference held in Bandung, Indonesia, in which representatives of over twenty-five Southern formations gathered to articulate the principles of the Non-Aligned Movement. Referencing Sukarno's speech at the opening of the conference, Prashad notes that these polities were united not by considerations of race or religion but by their "common detestation" of "colonialism... [and] racialism": although the "intense suspicion" of the Cold War era meant that such a platform ultimately didn't amount to much, it is worthy of emulation (144).

Although Prashad doesn't use the term, his work also constitutes a necessary provocation to the conceits of Han Chinese chauvinism—because it can help reduce the triumphalisms that we weave into our definitions of self. Posing the question "[w]hat would history look like from a polycultural perspective" and referencing in his response

---

2   Nusantara is the Javanese word for "archipelago." It references Singapore, Malaysia, Brunei, Indonesia, (Southern) Thailand, (Southern) Philippines, and Timor-Leste.

two prominent historians who study Confucianism, Prashad argues that, "rather than see Hong Kong business exclusively as a hybrid of an ancient Confucianism and a modern capitalism, as in the work of Tu Wei-ming, we might [then] take heed of the Jesuit role in the making of early modern 'Confucianism,' as in the fine work of Lionel Jensen" (67). For my purposes, this change in basic orientation is important because avoiding self-aggrandisement is a crucial first step for improving intergroup relations. Furthermore, this willingness to acknowledge the imbricated nature of the legacies we *actually* inherit also allows us to "snub the pretensions" of that ideology that arrogates to itself knowledge from different geo-cultural arenas but then proceeds to erase those contributions through amnesiac pronouncements on the achievements of "Western rationality" and "Western science" (often enough invoked to justify colonialism), a move that, as Prashad observes, "erases the influence of those Arab and Jewish scholars who extended Aristotle's insights, those Indian wizards who made mathematics possible with their discovery of the zero, [and] those Iroquois whose experiments with federalism helped frame some of the concepts for the U.S. Constitution" (67-68). For Prashad then (quoting the words of historian Robin Kelley):

> so-called 'mixed-race' children are not the only ones with a claim to multiple heritages. All of us, and I mean ALL of us, are the inheritors of European, African, Native American, and even Asian pasts, even if we can't exactly trace our bloodlines to all of these continents. (65)

As can be seen in the first indented quote above, Prashad is not endorsing elite forms of cosmopolitanism enjoyed by those safely ensconced in the upper circuits of globalization, or the consumerism that reduces complex lifeways to symbolic tokens available for use as ornamentation (e.g., Indo-chic, chinoiserie). The case studies that ground his claims are instead drawn from the class struggle and from anti-racist activism.

What supports Prashad's thesis is also its uptake in the field of social psychology as a new paradigm for comparative research of intergroup attitudes. In a 2012 study of several adult population groups in the United States, Rosenthal and Levy find, for instance, that "greater endorsement of polyculturalism was consistently associated with more positive intergroup attitudes" (2012: 11). This relationship held "for both dominant and marginalized groups" and its particulars included "[greater] appreciation for and comfort with diversity" as well as greater "*willingness for intergroup contact*" (1, 11). Building on the work of Prashad, Rosenthal and Levy, as well as others, Morris, Chiu and Liu also argue for the appositeness of the construal that our cultural traditions are "interacting systems" rather than separate genealogies (631). Because "[i]ndividuals take influences from multiple cultures" they also "become conduits through which cultures can affect each other" (631). And this suggests that literature also has a role to play by giving sensuous, believable detailing to the becoming-other that turns certain individuals into conduits, laying the groundwork then it would seem for *further* interaction and dialogue.

While Prashad sees polyculturalism as in some ways replacing multiculturalism, I would however advocate a more practicable mobilisation of *both* approaches, together with a third framework for construing diversity, namely colour-blindness, in line with Rosenthal's and Levy's suggestion in a 2010 paper that all three stances be taught in "educational settings" so that we can maximize the "strengths" and minimize the "weaknesses" of each position (2010: 215). Such a move views a strong emphasis on cultural boundedness as the historical and institutionally legitimised framework that polyculturalism needs to work both with and against to tackle the hazards of social fragmentation. For many individuals, a strong emphasis on (mono-)cultural heritage and allied notions of historical continuity does seem to compensate for the uncertainties generated by neoliberal capitalist modernity. Where the social reproduction of unequal difference occurs, it is also understandable that "strong" boundaries are maintained. To the extent that boundedness encourages people to live "parallel" lives, and to the extent that this may fuel prejudice and antipathy, however, a willingness for intergroup contact is also clearly important because it can help to improve social cohesion. Worth noticing also is Ganesan's implicit deployment of a polycultural frame when she discerns the assigning of an equal weight to "nature" as well as "nationalist[-exclusivist] and diasporic agencies" in the works she discusses. Unlike the identity politics or politics of recognition rehearsed by the latter two foci—one emphasising economic oppression, the other cultural-political oppression—nature appreciation and the sustainability ethos it fosters serves the common good because it maintains conditions of possibility needed for all to flourish. Since the authors she surveys are female, Ganesan's reading also implies that shared encounters with and resistance to patriarchy can animate intergroup solidarities. Rather than the current default, the mentioned politics of recognition pursued in the main by postcolonial studies, what the polycultural perspective encourages is thus a shift in interpretive foci to what we might call a politics of commonality that spotlights overlapping interests, projects, and concerns. As Prashad makes clear in his book, this entails a commitment to analysing cultures as historically interacting systems, connections, and convivialities, and not just as entities gripped by trials of contestation and self-avowal. Most importantly, the theoretical move that I am proposing is not to take the above as a settled argument. I suggest merely that we defer judgement on the feasibility or otherwise of "polyculturalism" while we return to the cultural archive and excavate texts with an eye to delineating the forms of socio-political commonality they may rehearse or endorse. An example that comes quickly to mind would be the works of the poet Salleh Ben Joned, who writes in Malay and English.

Before we can proceed, however, a brief excursus on nomenclature is needed in order to avoid confusion. While I share the reservations raised earlier about liberal multiculturalism's propensity to enshrine "tolerance" rather than transformative interchange, I do not adopt the category that Meer and Modood propose as a substitute, namely interculturalism. I think interculturalism and its cognate terms, hybridity or métissage, are better used to describe micro-processes pertaining to synthesis between "discrete" ethnic lifeways, a good example being the Sino-Malay creole culture that arose in earlier epochs when male Chinese migrants to Malaysia regularly practiced exogamy because of the paucity of female migrants from East Asia. Polyculturalism is for my purposes a more capacious category that includes "binary" processes as well as, for instance, the described interactions between English, Tamil, and Malay speech communities in *Between Lives*, and also the described interactions between English, Chinese, and Malay speech communities in *Days of Change*. "Manglish," the homegrown variety of English which shows ethnolectal contribution from several different tongues would be a good example of polyculturalism. In addition, I think it is necessary to distinguish our everyday understanding of (cultural) hybridity from its articulation within colonial discourse theory, where Lacanian analysis is used to render "hybridity" a paradigm of colonial anxiety, not a descriptor of postcolonial social realities (Bhabha, 1994). Finally, another term that needs to be briefly touched on here is transculturation. Popularised by Mary Louise Pratt, who uses it to denote "how subordinated or marginal groups select and invent from materials transmitted to them by a dominant or metropolitan culture" (6), transculturation appears to illuminate a number of South American contexts dominated by European cultural norms. However, this situation is arguably fundamentally different from Malaysia, where the imperative is to secure co-development of *different* Global South cultures rather than to tackle existential problematics tied intrinsically to the North-South divide.

Coalition Efforts

TO return to the matter at hand, I will elaborate in the sections below how *Between Lives* and *Days of Change* valorise the formation of polycultural "compacts" between individuals from different communities, instantiating in the process a politics of commonality.

Such compacts are needed because the scale of the challenge posed by the existential imperative to find sustainable lifeways means that all groups have to contribute. *Between Lives* (hereafter *Lives*) tells the story of Sellamma, an old woman of Indian heritage whose attachment to a plot of land "stretching from the laterite trail to the river and on to the fringes of a jungle" stands in the way of a developer's plans to build "a few blocks of condominiums, and a theme park" on it (1). Sumitra, who works for the government-run "Social Reconstruction Department" and who is also of Indian heritage, is sent to make her change her mind (1). To gain Sellamma's trust, Sumitra works alongside her in a fruit orchard cum vegetable garden adjoining her home. She allows Sellamma to believe that she is her lost/deceased sister, Anjalai, bathes naked with her in the river, and treks with her into the jungle. In more abstract terms, Sumitra participates in and fosters Sellamma's memory-cum-identity work as she narrates her life. A top performer in her department, Sumitra takes great pride in her "aloofness" from the "subjects" with whom she engages (8). As she enters Sellamma's orbit, however, it is, interestingly, she who undergoes a sea change.

In the process, readers sample an alternative, at times obscure, at times mystical worldview, one where it is not so much the land belonging to a person who gets to enjoy ownership rights, but where an individual belongs to the land, and thus has stewardship and conservation commitments. In effect, Sumitra undergoes a conversion experience. As she tills the vegetable plot with a hoe, working alongside Sellamma, the latter notes approvingly that "[y]our earth hands are coming back" (63). The possibility of a non-alienated relationship with the land also causes Sumitra to recall an "environmentalists'... song" that she hears often on the car radio, one stressing a "nurture-and-be-nurtured" mutuality between human beings and nature (63).

The reason for the bio-centric slant becomes clear as Sellamma recounts her growing up experiences before the outbreak of the Second World War. We learn that, having started out as a migrant rubber tapper, Sellamma's father had set up a homestead when his employer began to lay off workers, presumably because of a market slump. Newly enacted colonial administrative rules prohibited businesses from sending excess workers back to the "Big Country," which is to say, India, so the rubber company had helped them set up small land holdings (91). Sellamma's father was chosen to lead the way because he was literate, was in fact given to reading the Indian-Hindu epic *Ramayana*, and was seen as a leader or role model. Setting up home and planting food crops is framed as a figure for migrants putting down roots in a new homeland. Hence Sellamma's stubborn attachment to her surroundings.

For our purposes, the most provocative feature of *Lives* is the social compact it appends to the mentioned homesteading efforts.[3] This comes through in a key passage describing how a character named Pak Mat helps Sellamma's father set up the family's fruit orchard or "dusun," with the upshot that ecological reproduction is aligned with the reproduction of minority cultural life (109). An occasional provider of animal trapping, weed removal, and jungle-clearing services for the plantation that is releasing workers, Pak Mat, has been tasked to help with their transition to a new life:

> The land was already overflowing with mango, coconut, papaya, pineapple, sugar cane, besides bunds of Malaikaran [Malay], Cheenan [Chinese] and Indian vegetables such as pandan, serai, puchok, manis, lady's fingers, pumpkins, avarakai, chillie, brinjal, and murungakai. Now with the dusun Pak Mat was helping to start, they would have seasonal fruit trees: chiku, chempedak, jack fruit, mangosteen, rambutan, langsat, and of course, the most exotic of fruit, the durian! (109)

By juxtaposing local food crops with those brought over by migrant settlers, the text stresses *commensurability* between settler and

---

3   For an opposed reading stressing the essentialist investments of the novel, see Lim (2008).

autochthonous lifeways. "Pak" is a Malay word meaning "Sir" while "Mat" is an informal term referencing the autochthonous population. That a so-named character helps Sellamma's father, and also the fact that they later become firm friends, suggests that the enterprise of putting down roots is cast as a public good, a cross- or polycultural compact that initiates, preserves, and extends the benefits of mutuality. The use of literary multilingualism, with insertions of romanized Tamil ("Malaikaran," "Cheenan") and Malay words ("dusun") into the English text strengthens this meme. Furthermore, the fact that the durian, an iconic local fruit, is tagged as "exotic" suggests an attempt to loosen the native-settler distinction in the national cultural imaginary. Against the exclusionary pressures directed at settler communities, *Lives* stresses the bounteous, munificent nature of the tropical rainforest and lowland biome. It suggests that the key requirement for minority cultural reproduction is meaningful forms of localization.

What needs to be stressed here is the contingent rather than essentialist (or neo-traditionalist) gloss given to Pak Mat. For rather than grant nativist imprimatur to the homesteading efforts of Sellamma's father, an act that preserves the priority of the former, Pak Mat's legitimating function may be said to stem from his fruit-farming and outdoorsman skills, which is to say from his ability to forge a sustainable relationship with the land. The importance of sustainability is underlined by other details including the "[e]co-art" that Sellamma's late brother, Chinnathambi, makes or finds: these are fallen tree branches that he retrieves from the forest, a practice that implicitly censures modern-day consumerism (69). But most importantly it is the closure of *Lives* that most validates my argument, for it avers that meaningful levels of sustainability can only be achieved by all communities coming together in an extensive, new social compact. The closure follows Sellamma's signing of her landholdings to Sumitra just before she dies, the baton being passed to the latter. But rather than fight the unnamed developer threatening her lands on her own, Sumitra convinces two of her colleagues to join her: Mei, who is of Chinese heritage, and, Aishah, who is of Malay heritage, which means that the earlier compact between Sellamma's father and Pak Mat actually foreshadows this turn of events.

Earlier in the novel, Sumitra's and Sellamma's swim in the river had presaged Sumitra's transformation of perspective. As the novel closes, we are shown Mei, Aishah, and Sumitra swimming in the same stretch of river, undergoing it appears an analogous act of transformation. As the epigraph above suggests, submergence in water supplies an experience of corporeal boundaries "falling" away. The encounter with the sublime gestures at an attenuation of ethnic being, so that it is not skin colour that matters but "green-ness" or our common humanity. We might say that, as an iteration of eco-popular impulses, the polycultural coalition set up here exemplifies the trend towards "commonality" identified by Ganesan. It advances a national imaginary less riven by ethnic self-assertion. *Lives* ends with the three women putting the details of their struggle on the internet. They break the figurative fourth-wall as they address the reader, saying, "[t]his is the only way we can reach you—through our web site" (384). We are not told whether they succeed in fending off redevelopment, but the important point it would seem is the coalition they constructed, and the struggle that they're engaged in.

As shown above, the notion that shared conservation ideals can provide the basis for new forms of collective life is powerfully explored in *Lives*. Beyond the conservation ethic, however, the concrete details of what we might call alternative forms of development are not provided. This is where *Days of Change* and the remaining texts supply part of the answer, insofar as they gesture at indigenous and autochthonous forms of knowledge that can be deployed in the larger endeavour to secure social progress, while urging the formation of polycultural coalitions to aid that effort. *Days of Change* (hereafter *Days*) is conceptually or generically related to *Lives* in that it also presents a reversal story with existentialist implications. As mentioned, it tells the story of a property developer who "changes" sides rather than a bureaucrat fighting obstructive land use. Having made his fortune from, in essence, contributing to a "dirigiste" or state-led model of economic advancement, the developer, Hafiz, undergoes a sea-change analogous to Sumitra's when he falls down a ravine while on land inspection and wakes up suffering from amnesia in an isolated village named Kampung Basoh (Zainor 32). Cared for by two traditional healers named Pak Endoh and Mak Soh, Hafiz is impressed by their "professionalism" and grasp of traditional ecological knowledge (TEK) even as he is appalled by the crushing "poverty" that he sees around him and the fatalism that it breeds (99, 163). The formal academic term TEK is not used in the text, but the practices of the two healers, their vast knowledge of herbal pharmacology, and their "bone-sett[ing]" and therapeutic massage skills come under its domain (94). While Hafiz is eventually rescued after a sojourn in Kampong Basoh, his memories of its gemeinschaft setting and of the uncomplicated piety of Pak Endoh and Mak Soh cause him to reassess his priorities even as he ponders the antimonies between "tradition and modernity" (170).

As he undergoes what is in effect an existential and spiritual crisis, Hafiz begins to question his adherence to dominant notions of progress, these being "dream[s] conjured up . . . by a consumerist system," and also the "mindless pursuit of western definitions and standards of development" (152, 158). He recalls suddenly a conversation that he had with his gardener, Maniam, when the latter was being pressurised to abandon his lodgings in an urban squatter area earmarked for an office block cum shopping mall project. Like the other squatters, Maniam was slated to receive in return what Hafiz felt was "more than adequate compensation" for the "hovels" at issue, namely a new "brick and concrete" low-cost flat (157). But Maniam disabuses him of that presumption. As he explains:

> what developers and the government failed to grasp was that the hovels were surrounded by land on which the squatters could grow vegetables and small fruit-bearing trees, rear chickens, ducks, geese, perhaps a goat or two, or even a milk-cow—food, or sources of food, that kept them going on a day-to-day basis when money was scarce. Or that they could sell to supplement the day-

wages most of them earned. Move them to a low-cost flat,
and they would have to pay for everything they ate. Gone
would be the wild plants or parts of cultivated plants that
many city-dwellers hardly think of as food: male papaya
flowers, young tapioca shoots, banana flowers, and edible
convolvuli growing wild by the ditches. (157)

Arising from these deliberations, Hafiz decides to revive a
community project cherished by his father, Yusuf, one that he had
left dormant while chasing business goals. Instead of the "science
college" that his father wanted to establish, however, Hafiz proposes
to build a "college of traditional science" focused on the study of
"alternative medicine," preserving therein the TEK practices of Pak
Endoh and Mak Soh while validating the alternative epistemologies
they instantiate (167). With the college acting as a backdrop, Hafiz
imagines that Kampung Basoh could grow into a kind of "traditional
health village," a network of which could form the basis of a
"nationwide health- and eco-tourist industry" (168, 173). Among the
possibilities for expansion: members of the indigenous community
called "*orang asli*" can act as "guides" for the jungle treks arranged
in the eco-tourism itineraries (168); the health villages can feature
"botanical garden[s] of trees and plants used in traditional medicine,"
and specialists such as "botanists [and] biochemists" can also
be hired so that TEK treatments are "tested, documented, and
systematised" (167).

In a plot twist that functions as a warning against investment in
untenable notions of ecotopia and regressive "populist" nostalgia,
Hafiz discovers however that his recollection of Kampung Basoh
was actually a false-memory. Rather than a protracted stay in a so-
named village, he had actually spent six months in hospital in a coma
after his fall down the ravine. Hafiz experiences a breakdown after
the discovery and questions his sanity. After recovering, he decides
nevertheless that his scheme is worth pursuing, and as such ropes
in his cousin, Ai Lian, who is of Chinese heritage, and niece, Anna,
who is of mixed Chinese-European heritage, to join his project. As

in *Lives*, the concluding polycultural compact set up here suggests that the know-how and resources of all communities have a role to play in discovering and promoting sustainable lifeways. Anna we are told used to run a landscaping business; Ai Lian has knowledge of investment and financing. As in *Lives*, *Days* also foreshadows this development by enacting an earlier compact between members of different communities. This occurs when some of his hometown denizens try to rope Hafiz into a NIMBY protest against plans to turn a nearby forest reserve into a "cartoon theme park," one that would be "bigger and better and more state-of-the-art than anything the country had yet seen" (84). In a memorable iteration of the eco-popular, we see members of both settler and autochthonous communities joining the protest effort, which attracts an assortment of working professionals and retirees. While taking the form of the journal writings of a Malay Muslim man, that is, of Hafiz, *Days* is also marked by the intriguing use of hexagrams taken from the Chinese *Book of Changes*, with different hexagrams from the classic acting as epigraphs for different sections of the text, thus underscoring through *both* form and content the polyculturality that is at issue.

Common Dreams

AS can be seen above, *Lives* and *Days* advance a politics of commonality that I would argue doesn't necessarily invalidate a strong "culture-bound" interpretive foci, since they also clearly pursue, respectively, Malaysian-Indian and Malaysian-Chinese concerns. Since my analysis only tackles Anglophone texts, I am, however, vulnerable to the charge of making an insidious claim, of suggesting that only MLE works have the expansive horizons needed to enact modes of polyculturalism. To forestall this accusation, I would like to turn now to two MLC texts that, I claim, also highlight polycultural considerations. Like the Anglophone texts, the following works underline the need for cooperation and mutuality between minority and majoritarian communities even in the face of tensions and dissensus. But concomitantly they also appreciate that such goals cannot be accomplished if hermetic notions of culture pressed by neo-traditionalism are not tackled and dispelled. The first MLC work that I would like to discuss is a short story by Li Zishu titled "Northern Country Borderlands" (hereafter "Borderlands"). Told eerily in the second person, "Borderlands" is the lead story in Li's 2010 short story collection, *Rogue Buddha*. It concerns a twenty-nine-year-old Malaysian-Chinese protagonist named Chen who fights a curse that afflicts the men of his family, causing them all to die young before they reach the age of thirty. The curse began from the time of his great-grandfather, who, shortly after arriving in Southeast Asia from China, had killed a "strange-looking beast" for food, offending as a result a "mountain goblin-spirit" which placed the curse on him and his male offspring (21).[4] The deaths of Chen's great-grandfather, grandfather, father, uncle, and several of his grand-uncles are all attributed to the curse.

To escape the affliction, Chen needs to find a fabled "dragon-tongue" herb mentioned in testimonies and records left behind by his father and great-grandfather (19, 37). His main clue is his father's journal which details his search for the plant, and which also contains between its leaves the mentioned records. Chen's research into the affliction leads him to consult a Chinese encyclopaedic dictionary published in 1915 called "Cihai" (23). The narration also weaves in other instantiations of the Chinese cultural archive including a classic sixteenth-century herbological text called the "Compendium of Materia Medica" as well as a "Chinese herbal illustrative compendium" (20, 28). As Chen approaches his thirtieth birthday, the symptoms of the affliction—falling hair, searing pains and cramps, uncontrolled sweating, palpitations, migraines, nightmares, hallucinations, and even a mania to chew wood—get progressively worse. Chen returns to his hometown situated in the northernmost part of the country near the Thai border and searches for the plant in the area near where his father's cadaver was found at the mouth

---

4   All quotes from this and the following story are my own translations from the original.

of a nearby river. He has a vague memory of searching thereabouts with his father for the herb, of achieving some success in an isolated unnamed "ravine" when he was a young boy (19, 30). At his father's funeral, Chen had found in his clenched palm the remnants of one of the sought-after plants, which his father apparently did not have time to imbibe, so he is convinced that his memories of encountering it have some basis in reality. He enlists members of the indigenous population to help him find the ravine, and also consults the gatherers who come to the area to harvest Tongkat Ali, a highly-prized local aphrodisiac-herb; but all his efforts are in vain.

Eventually after suffering great hardship—and with the affliction increasingly impeding his movement and grip on consciousness—Chen finds the dragon-tongue herb in an isolated marshy river. He discovers that it is not a conventional plant with normal roots but a semi-aquatic, "parasite-[type]" plant with "hollow" stalks that can draw sustenance from micro-organisms found in water (35). After he recovers, Chen sets out to find out more about a half-brother whom he only learned about recently. The existence of the brother is revealed in a handwritten plea written on the back of his father's will. From the note, Chen learns that his father, in a bout of dissipation caused by the affliction, had had a tryst with a Malaysian-Chinese widow and had gotten her with child, a son who, after he was born, was given up in adoption to a man who ran a business making Chinese funeral caskets. Any of his progeny who survive the curse should also help this son, Chen's father pleads in his message. Chen discovers that his half-brother was not, however, brought up in the casket maker's family. He was instead given up in adoption again to a Malay family because the wife of the casket maker found him too "swarthy": his "large mouth" and "thick lips" made her suspect that he was of a foreign or "external ethnicity" (36). Chen goes to his half-brother's residence, a Malay-style house on stilts, and begins talking to his wife. From framed photographs hung on the wall, Chen learns that his half-brother was brought up a Muslim and had gone on pilgrimage to Mecca. He is three years older than Chen so the latter expects that he has died from the family affliction.

To his surprise, however, Chen learns that he is alive. He makes a comfortable living selling homeopathic and beauty products derived from Tongkat Ali, so it is presumably the imbibing of this herb that saved his life. In an implicit rebuke to the authority of Chinese herbalism, and, by implication, the neo-traditionalism performed by the archival instantiations cited above, "Borderlands" tells us that Chen's half-brother is actually in much better state than him. Chen is emaciated and frail whereas his half-brother is robust and hale: he has, in fact, three wives and eight children. Chen leaves the house when his questions about his half-brother's health upsets his wife and she shouts—ironically given the context—"Why do you Chinese people like to curse other people!" (38). Before he leaves, Chen buys a box of Tongkat Ali ointment from the wife. He elects to stay on in the town. As the story ends, he sees a doppelganger or secret sharer figure walking towards him, one that resembles a personification of death encountered earlier in the text.

As can be seen, "Borderlands" is a rich, suggestive text whose *primary* plot twist—the half-brother's surmounting of the putative family curse—shows up the limitations of hermetic notions of identity. The text foreshadows this denouement when it provides at one point a detail about the Chinese businesses operating in the town: "Tongkat Ali is a herb that belongs to the Malays; but much like Malay traditional healers, Traditional Chinese Medicine practitioners in the town also revere its medicinal properties" (29). The town also has two Chinese restaurants selling game whose liberal use of the aphrodisiac-herb allow them to do a roaring trade, with the text noting that its devotees are, as it were, "converts" to a beguiling new set of beliefs (30). Although culinary hybridity is only an initial step in the development of meaningful polyculturality, it would seem that "Borderlands" invites us to compare its endorsement of *difference* with the racial exclusion enunciated by the casket maker's wife. The fact that her family gets its income from selling coffins would seem to be a figurative way of stating that ethnocentrism is a dead-end. That Chen's father gives to the half-brother the Chinese name "Guan Hong," which means wide or "great vision," further points to the story's rejection of chauvinism (36). In this concern, the title of the story—emphasising the crossing of borders by those who come from Southern Thailand to Malaysia to gather the Tongkat Ali herb—may be said to emphasize the ordinariness of cultural border-crossing. Because it acts as a metonym for culture, the fact that the dragon-tongue plant is itself semi-aquatic in nature and can drift on water would then further undermine the assumption that cultural borders must of needs be impermeable. In this regard, Chen's failure to find the "ravine" where he first encountered the dragon-tongue herb—or so he believes—arguably operates in the same way as Hafiz's mis-remembering of Kampung Basoh in *Days*. They both register the limitations attending neo-traditional construals of self and the other.

Forest Scripts

OUR final text, "Prey," is by Hai Fan, and appeared in his 2017 short story collection, *Delicious Hunger*. "Prey" is constructed as three separate mini-stories with different protagonists. Each of them stresses the importance of sustainability and human-nature relationality, thus raising trenchantly the question of what constitutes the "common good." Before elaborating on these features, however, I should add that Hai Fan is by citizenship a Singapore writer. I place his work here nonetheless because it draws on his thirteen-year experience as a soldier fighting with the Malayan Communist Party (MCP) in the jungles of northern peninsular Malaysia, the stint ending in 1989 when he resumed civilian life following the signing of the historic Hatyai peace accord. While Hai Fan didn't settle down in Malaysia, he risked his life for ideals held by many Malaysians, including those in the MCP's tenth Malay regiment, whose members were predominantly Malay, and which is referenced indeed at one point in the collection (see "Wild Mangoes"). As the world retreats from the absolutisms of the Cold War, the proposition that the MCP's post-Second World War activities were anti-colonial rather than narrowly communitarian in scope has gained ground, a stance bolstered it would seem by its earlier anti-Occupation efforts.

To the extent that many Malaysian-Chinese view the retrieval of this historical understanding as crucial to a judicious appreciation of their collective contribution to national formation, Hai Fan's writing aids that effort. Furthermore, as Li Zishu herself notes in a foreword to the collection, Hai Fan's writing stands out among most or even all of the works produced by former MCP fighters-turned-writers because it doesn't carry a "propagandistic" tone inhibiting circulation and acceptance (Li 2017: 7). "Regrettably," therefore, he "may well be . . . the only one" among this coterie of writers who has both the literary skills and experiential-heft needed to make that era come to life (Li 2017: 9).

Even so, Hai Fan stresses in a recent interview that his works should be termed "rainforest writing" rather than "MCP writing," one of their aims being to challenge the insidious notion that the rainforest is a "gruesome" place full of "terror" and "fear" (Hai Fan, qtd. in Gan 71, 73). Instead, Hai Fan insists, the rainforest is a place of "amity, joie de vivre [and] gracefulness" (Hai Fan, qtd. in Gan 73). Arising from this orientation, all the stories in *Delicious Hunger* inclusive of the three "Prey" mini-stories contain passages of great beauty celebrating human-nature engagement. They are not "war" stories in the conventional sense of the term, seeking instead to communicate an ecological anagnorisis gleaned from long residence in the jungle, that being a repudiation of the general cultural "ecophobia" (Estok, 2018) that fosters environmental despoliation. To the question of what constitutes the common good, therefore, the answer provided by "Prey" is its commitment to a politics of commonality advanced through a conservation and stewardship agenda.

Returning to the work under discussion, "Yellow Muntjac," the first mini-story of "Prey," describes two MCP cadres who are out hunting. One of them, Ah Na, is from the "Senoi" tribe, one of the indigenous peoples of Malaysia (107). The other, Keding, who is of Chinese ethnicity, marvels at how he often "learns new things" when he sets out with his indigenous comrades, including in this instance how to set a trap properly and how to bury game in the soil so that it can be retrieved unspoilt at the end of the hunt (108). Apart from hunting skills, Ah Na also teaches Keding how to munch certain kinds of leaves that leave an invigorating aftertaste in the mouth. A while later, they chance upon a muntjac (a kind of deer) caught in a trap just at the point where it gnaws off one of its limbs and runs away. When Keding gives chase, however, Ah Na stops him. He shares with him a Senoi belief that forest creatures will, in extremis, deploy dangerous "secret weapons" to defend themselves, so it is safer not to continue the hunt: his brother had apparently experienced that trait once while chasing a porcupine (111). Although surprised, Keding elects to follow Ah Na's decision because of the latter's attitude of reverence and fear as he recounts this item of belief. Nevertheless, the turn of events leaves him stunned and confounded.

The issue of assigning strict, regulative principles to human-nature interaction is also staged in the second mini-story "Black Bear," which starts with two female members of an eight-person agriculture unit checking on the game traps they had set up earlier. Spotting a bear in one of the traps, one of them, Dan Xiu, shoots it dead. Realising that the bear is a cub, and figuring that the mother will come back for it, they decide to set another trap with the dead cub as bait. If they kill the mother, each member of their unit would have a bear paw that can be used to make traditional Chinese tonics or remedies. When Dan Xiu later sets out to check on the trap, however, Yan Hua, who had accompanied her earlier, is assigned to sentry duty. She learns subsequently that the mother bear did come back for the cub and was killed by Dan Xiu. When the paws are distributed, however, Yan Hua refuses to take her share. Her portion should go to the "public purse" or to Dan Xiu, she says (119). Yan Hua doesn't take her share because, as often happened, she was assaulted by memories of her partner and child while on guard duty. Her partner had died a few years earlier during an ambush conducted by joint Thai-Malaysian forces. Their son was left behind in a village a day after he was born, just before they both joined the struggle. As Yan Hua struggles with these memories she also reminisces about her parents. Her refusal to take her share of the spoils thus stems from an awareness of kindred-ness. She connects the behaviour of the bear returning for its cub with her own loss and sacrifice. It is her own grasping after an ethical universal that would make sense of her experience that sustains this rendition of cross-speciesism, her understanding that her own pining for her son and parents is violated if she takes the bear paw. Furthermore, her experience of losing her partner in an ambush allows her to understand to the fullest extent what it means to be the titular prey of the story.

A continuation of this train of thought—the vulnerability of MCP fighters highlighting the vulnerability of nature—is also seen in the final mini-story "Mousedeer." The story begins with news going around the encampment that someone named Ai Yue has captured a mousedeer, the Chinese term itself, " 本蘭鹿 " ("Ben Lan Lu") being a transliteration of the creature's Malay name "pelanduk," which is actually given in Roman script in the text (120). While working in the underground in Singapore before she joined the struggle in the rainforest, Ai Yue's selfless devotion to her cause had badly damaged her health, and now her poor constitution means she is often a hindrance to her comrades. She often disturbs their sleep at night with her coughing, is unable to take on many duties, has odd and eccentric ways, gets into unnecessary quarrels, and is often lost in her thoughts. The mini-story ends with Ai Yue releasing the mousedeer. She seems to see aspects of herself in the creature, for like it, she is weak, secretive, and isolated. More positively, however, Ai Yue also references its status in Malay folk culture, where it is celebrated for being able to use its wiles and intelligence to consistently outwit the nasty "crocodile" (121). Although unsaid, she is like the mousedeer fighting the crocodile, someone who can only rely on her wiles and intelligence.

As can be seen, all three mini-stories of "Prey" refuse to confine animals to the realm of *zoe* or bare life, to that which is killable, to use the term proposed by Agamben. In so doing, "Prey" gestures at the need to move beyond speciesism: it critiques the hyper-separation of the human socio-cultural realm from the realm tagged as "nature." For my purposes, however, the striking feature here is the way in which these properly "ecological" concerns are delineated through expansive encounters with indigenous and Malay folkways, and also through critique of one's own traditional belief system. Like *Lives*, literary multilingualism is used in "Mousedeer" to express affiliation with the majoritarian community. In contrast to the Marxist doxa that might have proclaimed tribal lifeways backward and retrograde, "Yellow Muntjac" opts to register their nature-directed awe and reverence. "Black Bear" in turn underscores the need to modernise lay beliefs about the restorative value of imbibing animal parts. In sum, we might say, "Green" thought is evidently important in the present context of eco-crisis, but on top of that, as "Prey" and the epigraph above suggests, it can also help us navigate the problematics of ethnic particularity by spotlighting commonplace human fallibility redeemed by fellow-feeling and companionableness.

To return to the engagement suggested in the introduction, the theoretical propaedeutic that I am proposing is inscribed in the methodology deployed in the present essay. The task at hand is to re-visit the cultural archive with a view to identifying the modes, modalities, and forms of polyculturalism inscribed in them—exactly in the manner done so here—so that we can register positive cultural engagement—a politics of commonality—and not just conflict or tension. While my language capabilities limit me to texts written in English and Chinese, there are certainly many scholars who can widen the scope of the present discussion by engaging texts written in other languages. The key consideration, I think, is that we must undertake *comparative* analyses of fiction written in different languages, since it is difficult to see how monological conceptions of culture can be weakened if we attend only to literature drawn from a single speech community. Such work will not fully displace the "myths" of cultural purity that permeate public life and our everyday interactions. But it may help reduce the appeal of the neo-traditionalist nostrums animating xenophobia and Islamophobia in the West and social exclusion in the global South.

WORKS CITED

Bhabha, Homi K. (1994) *The Location of Culture* (New York & London: Routledge).

Chuah Guat Eng (2010) *Days of Change: A Malaysian Novel* (Kuala Lumpur: Holograms).

Estok, Simon C. (2018) *The Ecophobia Hypothesis* (New York & London: Routledge).

Gan Jia Joe (2019) "Hai Fan's Communist Party of Malaya Writings to Rainforest Writings." Graduation thesis, School of Humanities, Nanyang Technological University.

Ganesan, Kavitha (2019) "Nature in Contemporary Malaysian Life-Writings in English." *Journal of Postcolonial Writing* 55.2 (May): 169-181.

Hai Fan (2017) *Kekou de Jie* [*Delicious Hunger*] (Petaling Jaya, Selangor: Got One Publisher).

Li Zishu (2010) *Ye Pusa* [*Rogue Buddha*] (Taipei: Linking Publishing Company).

Li Zishu (2017) "Sizhu, Cangliang, Zuori zhi Ren" [Dead Pigs, Hidden Food, and Men of Yesterday]. Hai Fan (2017): 5-10.

Lim, David C.L. (2008) "'Your Memories Are Our Memories': Remembering Culture as Race in Malaysia and K.S. Maniam's *Between Lives*." David C.L. Lim (ed.): *Overcoming Passion for Race in Malaysia Cultural Studies* (Leiden: Brill), 153-166.

Luke, Timothy W. (1999) *Capitalism, Democracy, and Ecology: Departing from Marx* (Illinois: University of Illinois Press).

Maniam, K.S. (2013) *Between Lives* (Petaling Jaya: Maya Press).

Meer, Nasar & Tariq Modood (2012) "How Does Interculturalism Contrast with Multiculturalism?" *Journal of Intercultural Studies* 33.2: 175-196.

Morris, Michael W., Chiu Chi-yue & Liu Zhi (2015) "Polycultural Psychology." *Annual Review of Psychology* 66.1: 631-659.

Prashad, Vijay (2001) *Everybody Was Kung Fu Fighting: Afro-Asian Connections and the Myth of Cultural Purity* (Boston: Beacon).

Pratt, Mary Louise (1992) *Imperial Eyes* (New York & London: Routledge).

Rosenthal, Lisa & Sheri R. Levy (2010) "The Colorblind, Multiculture, and Polycultural Ideological Approaches to Improving Intergroup

Attitudes and Relations." *Social Issues and Policy Review* 4.1: 215-246.

Rosenthal, Lisa & Sheri R. Levy (2012) "The Relation Between Polyculturalism and Intergroup Attitudes Among Racially and Ethnically Diverse Adults." *Cultural Diversity and Ethnic Minority Psychology* 18.1: 1-16.

Zainor Izat Zainal (2014) "Malaysia's Development Success Story: Critical Responses in Contemporary Malaysian Novels in English." *Asian Culture and History* 6.1: 31-42.

AFTERWORD

TEE Kim Tong

> And the dark man
> In their bloody work, who will come yet if we stay,
> Or if we run and are running everywhere.
>
> ——Shirley Geok-lin Lim, "Sugar-Cane"

IN May 13-14, 2019, the Center for the Humanities of National Sun Yat-sen University hosted a symposium on "Post-513 Malaysian Literatures and Cultural Articulations." The key phrase "May 13 Incident" refers to the racial riots that took place in Kuala Lumpur on the Thirteenth of May, 1969 and days after. In the riots residential and shop houses were burnt and hundreds of people, exact numbers still unknown, were killed and most of the victims were ethnic Chinese. A state of emergency was declared, curfew announced, parliament suspended, and subsequently National Operation Council was formed to run the country until 1971. The communal conflict had, in fact, opened a new chapter in the history of Malaysia as the government soon restructured the multiracial country into a Malay dominant state by implementing the New Economic Policy, National Culture Policy, and Malay-favored educational quota system. Instead of restructuring the society, these policies have made Malaysia "a country divided," a country whose population is categorized bifurcately as Bumiputras and Non-Bumiputras. Ironically, this racialized ideology is, in fact, a repetition of the country's ex-colonialist strategy of divide-and-rule.

More than fifty years have elapsed since the May 13 Riots, but no judicial redress of the massive victimization has been made. Quantity-wise, there are only few Malaysian literary and cultural articulations as well as representations of the May 13 Incident. Perhaps such a phenomena reflects our fear, our shame, and our failure——fear for another wave of riots, shame because such an incident took place in our country, which we claim to be democratic, multiracial, and multicultural, and failure because we were unable to uphold our belief in justice and righteousness.

To re-memory the May 13 Incident that happened more than fifty years ago, or rather, to exorcise the ghosts that have since haunted the country for so long a time, so that we could reframe our history and call for truth and reconciliation, we need to re-open the seal of the closed case. The May 13-14, 2019 international symposium we held four years ago was meant to be an act of reinscribing our collective memory.

During the two days of the symposium, twenty-one papers, in Chinese and English, were presented and a keynote speech was delivered by scholars of literature from Malaysia, Singapore, United States, and Taiwan. Presenters discussed Sinophone, Anglophone, and Malay texts by fiction writers and poets such as Liang Yuan, Fang Tian, Ho Sok Fong, Li Zishu, Looi Yook Tho, Ding Yun, Li Tianbao, Shirley Geok-lin Lim, Chuah Guat Eng, Shahnon Ahmad, Abdullah Hussain, Hanna Alkaf, Teo Tsu-Ming, and Preeta Samarasan. The cultural issues addressed by the papers presented include on-campus literary and academic activities, cultural identity, memory texts, media representation, postcolonial interpretation, trauma and post-trauma, politics of language, polyculturalism, oral history, and student movement.

This collection, *The Malaysian Albatross*, a title borrowed from Malachi Edwin Vethamani's essay topic, is not a proceeding of the symposium. The four essays collected here have been published respectively in issues No. 48 and No. 49 of *Sun Yat-sen Journal of Humanities* in 2020. In September 2021, seven papers from the symposium were published in the no. 43 issue of *Reflexion* [*Sixiang*], a Taipei-based journal published by the Linking Press. In fact, among the four essays we have gathered here, two were translated into Chinese and published in the *Reflexion*'s Special Topic on May 13 Incident.

Although for some reason the publication of this collection was delayed, I am glad that now I have come to the point of writing this afterword. I wish to thank all the paper presenters and participants of the symposium. I am grateful for the assistance of friends and colleagues at the Center for the Humanities, NSYSU when we hosted the symposium. Thanks must also go to Hsu Yan-tzu, Song Yu-chi, Dawn Hsieh, and Huang Shih-hao, my assistants who help the preparation and typesetting of this book at various stages. I would like, finally, to thank Wai Chew for co-editing with me.

TEE Kim Tong
Kaohsiung, 2023

LIST OF CONTRIBUTORS

Shirley Geok-lin LIM

Professor Emerita, University of California, Santa Barbara; Visiting Professorships at MIT, NUS, National Sun Yat-sen University, Chair Professor HKU. Her research fields cover creative writing pedagogy, and postcolonial, feminist, and ethnic American studies. Winner of the Commonwealth Poetry Prize for *Crossing the Peninsula*; two American Book Awards; and the Multiethnic Literatures of the United States (MELUS) and Feminist Press Lifetime Achievement Awards, she has published in *Hudson Review*, *Feminist Studies*, *Virginia Quarterly Review*, etc.; a memoir, *Among the White Moon Faces*; eleven poetry collections, most recently *In Praise of Limes*; three novels; *The Shirley Lim Collection*; and three story collections.

Malachi Edwin VETHAMANI

A Malaysian Indian poet, writer, editor, critic, bibliographer, and Emeritus Professor at University of Nottingham. He has published five collections of poems: *Rambutan Kisses* (2022), *The Seven O'clock Tree* (2022), *Love and Loss* (2022), *Life Happens* (2017) and *Complicated Lives* (2016). He has also published a collection of short stories, *Coitus Interruptus and Other Stories* (2018). His research on Malaysian literature in English led to the publication of *A Bibliography of Malaysian Literature in English* (2015) and two edited volumes of Malaysian writings in English, *Malchin Testament: Malaysian Poems* (2018) and *Ronggeng-Ronggeng: Malaysian Short Stories* (2020). Both these two volumes cover over sixty years of Malaysian writing in English. The Malaysian Publishers Association awarded *Malchin Testament: Malaysian Poems* the National Book Award 2020 for the English Language category. He is Founding Editor of *Men Matters Online Journal* (December 2020).

Florence KUEK

Senior Lecturer at the Department of Chinese Studies, Faculty of Arts & Social Sciences, University of Malaya. Her research foci include Malaysian literary studies, literary criticism, and educational research. Her latest indexed publications include a critical study on the AI literature in Malaysian Chinese literature (2022) and, re-reading of "Han Suyin's Picnic in Malaya" in the newly independent Malaya (2021), among others. She is also involved in Malay, English, and Chinese translation works. Her translated book titled *Tasik itu Bagai Cermin: Antologi Cerpen Sastera Mahua* (2022) introduces Malaysian Chinese literature to Malay-language readers.

SIM Wai Chew

Associate Professor of English in the School of Humanities at Nanyang Technological University, Singapore. He is the co-editor of *Island Voices: A Collection of Short Stories from Singapore* and *British-Asian Fiction: Framing the Contemporary*. He also recently authored an English translation of a Singaporean Sinophone novel titled *Exile or Pursuit*, and his research interests include Postcolonial Literature and Comparative Literature.

TEE Kim Tong (editor)

A retired Professor and an adjunct research fellow at National Sun Yat-sen University, Kaohsiung, Taiwan. His research areas cover Comparative Literature, Anglophone and Sinophone Southeast Asian Literature, and Translation Studies. His recent publications include *Literary Formations: Sinophone/Anglophone Malaysian Literature and Diasporic Identity* (2021), an English translation of Singaporean poet-artist Tan Swie Hian's Chinese poems, *Tan Swie Hian: Selected Poems 1964-1997* (2021), and a collection of critical essays, *By the Side of Charles River: Essays on Sinophone Malaysian Literature* (in Chinese, 2022). He is also editor of many collections of *Mahua* fiction and critical works on the Sinophone Malaysian literature.

CONTENTS